My Truth

The far-memory of Christopher Marlowe

by
Brenda Harwood

Bloomington, IN  Milton Keynes, UK
authorHOUSE®

AuthorHouse™
1663 Liberty Drive, Suite 200
Bloomington, IN 47403
www.authorhouse.com
Phone: 1-800-839-8640

AuthorHouse™ UK Ltd.
500 Avebury Boulevard
Central Milton Keynes, MK9 2BE
www.authorhouse.co.uk
Phone: 08001974150

© 2006 Brenda Harwood. All rights reserved.

No part of this book may be reproduced, stored in a retrieval system, or transmitted by any means without the written permission of the author.

First published by AuthorHouse 8/21/2006

ISBN: 1-4259-3393-9 (sc)

Printed in the United States of America
Bloomington, Indiana

This book is printed on acid-free paper.

Table of Contents

Foreword ix
I Live Again.. xiii
Introduction... xv

Chapter 1
My home life and schooldays in Canterbury 1

Chapter 2
University years... 19

Chapter 3
The Playmaker... 39

Chapter 4
The Babington Plot 49

Chapter 5
Peter Basconi... 65

Chapter 6
The Bradley affray 75

Chapter 7
Living with Thomas Kydd.. 79

Chapter 8
Robert Poley 87

Chapter 9
Sir Walter Raleigh... 95

Chapter 10
Thomas Walsingham and Scathebury............................ 105

Chapter 11
The Rose... 113

Chapter 12
Sir Roger Manwood.. 117

Chapter 13
The School of Night.. 119

Chapter 14
My visits to Scotland with Sweet Robin 129

Chapter 15
Coining in Flushing 131

Chapter 16
The Last Act 135

Chapter 17
Deptford 151

Far memory by Kit
   3rd March 1998 155
Epilogue 159

Dedication

I dedicate this book to my cousin Geoffrey Bird, who passed away in July 2003, much beloved by all.

I also would like to thank family and friends who have stood firmly by my side through the writing of this book.

Foreword

For those interested in the phenomenon of past life experience, either in the guise of therapist led imagery, be it hypnosis, Reiki, meditation or other method.

It could also be what has become known as 'far memory' or flashbacks. These can take the form of dreamlike images that can be repetitive, and can come complete with sound, colour and emotion. These flashbacks may begin in early childhood, often causing distress and confusion.

The author of this book, Brenda Harwood contacted me after watching a programme of Past Life Regression on ITVs 'This Morning', with Richard Madeley and the late Caron Keating.

Brenda was convinced that she had a positive knowledge of the personal life of Christopher Marlowe through insights that she had been given. At that time Brenda had no knowledge of the nature of past life regression or far memory. I advised her to read the books of A J Stewart, who has lived her life in Edinburgh as James IV of Scotland. Her books, 'Falcon', the autobiography of His Grace, James the Fourth, King of Scots and 'King's Memory', an autobiography of A J Stewart herself.

I first met AJ, as she liked to be called, at the launch party for 'King's Memory' in Glasgow on the 23 November 1982. I was impressed by her regal bearing, her glossy red hair, dressed in a long flowing dark robe and wearing a Falcon brooch on her breast. She claimed the brooch was the original, once worn by James himself!

I was first made aware of her story by the BBC who were making a documentary on Past Lives, featuring The Dalai Lama, the late Judge Christmas Humphries, who claimed to have been a Cathar in Spain in a past life and had been tortured and put to death by the Inquisition. The producer of the documentary suggested that I should go to Edinburgh to meet with AJ, take her through a regression to try to verify that her story was true …!

I saw no reason to subject the lady to this procedure, and despite originally agreeing to submit to hypnosis, she called off the experiment at the last minute. In my mind she had nothing to prove …!

AJ was born in the village of Tottington in the County Palatine of Lancaster. From an early age she saw images of steel-clad men with swords and axes, ships in convoy, and when she made mention to her parents of why she saw the images, "I was there", was her consistent reply.

The family name was Kay, but AJ always felt drawn to the surname Stewart and was eventually destined to wed someone of that name …

AJ eventually served in the ATS after the last war and found herself billeted in Edinburgh where she felt spiritually at home. She became a Scottish Nationalist, and all of this time had flashbacks of James's life.

The most powerful image was of one where she appeared to by lying on her back …; looking up at helmeted heads surrounding her, with staves and swords pointing down at her.

I met the lady on many occasions and we discussed the life of James and how it affected her. On one occasion I asked her what they ate in those far-off days. "Venison" was her reply, "but I am not allowed to stay in the kitchen to baste it". Such duties were not for a prince of the realm ...!!!

Another staple food was 'squab', which is actually pigeon or dove, and there were many lofts in Stirling Castle to hold the birds. She could remember the taste of the fowl, but could never recapture the flavour in this life, until she ventured into an Indian restaurant and had chicken cooked in saffron. I wondered if in fact such spices were available in Scotland in the 14th and 15th centuries and spoke to an historian that I was collaborating with on a story about the Great Drain surrounding Paisley Abbey. The Drain had been covered over, and although in times past it had been used as a moat in defence of the Abbey, it had fallen into disuse. There had been some excavations early this century and some artefacts and seeds discovered. One of the ingredients was in fact saffron ... So even then the preservative properties of the spice was understood.

It was only when AJ finally visited the battlefield of Flodden where James lost his life that she made the final connection. She walked around a small church, passed through a wicket gate at the rear and entered the field for the first time in this life. When she reached the part of the field that James died on, she once again had the image of a ring of faces above her, and tunnel of swords and staves arcing down towards her. She finally knew what the image meant. Enlightened, she made her way back up the hill, passed through the wicket gate and back into the Twentieth century.

The story of Kit Marlowe has similarly intrigued me since Brenda and I first met. We have had many conversations and innumerable letters. I have spoken directly to the character Marlowe for many hours, he is always gracious, well mannered and has an intellect far beyond what I might have expected from someone who lived in the time he did. Look at him another way, is this the man who gave us the timeless plays attributed to Shakespeare. Marlowe's occult knowledge, gained from his association with Dr John Dee, the alleged Queen's Conjurer, Sir Walter Raleigh and others in the School of Night, accepted as being one of the earliest Witchcraft Covens. I look forward to, in the future holding other conversations with the 16th century occultist, learning more of his relationship with the Bard of Stratford and his other more clandestine activities.

I leave you with this observation. This is Brenda's story. It is not a tale produced by some hypnotherapist desperate to create belief in past life regression. You must always remember that a good therapist can produce images in a susceptible subject that can appear to be a past life!!

Tom Barlow

I Live Again

Four centuries have passed,
Since Deptford town it was
Said I breathed my last.
For in my place another was laid,
To take my place, thus sealing my fate.
In a shroud of mystery, I left that place.
Many a tale was told of me, after I
Had left to go beyond the sea.
A forgotten man I became, writing
Under another's name, Sweet
Will upon thee I bestowed my fame,
But you are not to blame.

I passed away in secrecy, passed away
Upon a sunny springtime day.
No mother, father could mourn for me,
To help set this broken spirit free.
In sorrow and guilt my soul could not rest,
For the pain was too great within my breast.
The Spirit World could not comfort me,
So they decided to set me free.
To this new Elizabethan Age I came,
But not this time seeking fame,
For the truth about me I want to tell,
Yes, about my shame and living hell.

I grew without knowledge of my past,
Until one day it came clear at last.
When I saw a play about Sweet Will,
How Christopher Marlowe they did kill.
This I could not accept as true,
To put this right I know I must do.
My answers they revealed the clue,
To what happened that fateful day,
At Eleanor Bull's house on the 30th of May.

Brenda Harwood, 21 December 1993

Introduction

I was born on the 24 June 1949 in St Helens, Merseyside and when only a few months old I moved with my parents to live with my grandparents in Blackpool, Lancashire. My father was in the American Air Force and when I was about two years old my parents split up. As I grew the doctor discovered that I had an eye disability called nystagmus (involuntary movement of the eye ball), which sadly hindered my education and I didn't attend school until I was about seven years old. It was difficult at school, as there was not the help or the understanding for children with special needs then. But despite all this, I muddled through.

All through my school life, although I desperately wanted to learn, I was ridiculed by teachers and made fun of by other children because my eyes were unable to focus. But I remained strong in mind and ignored their lack of knowledge.

Time moved on and I became a carer for the elderly, which I found to be rewarding although not my chosen career path. One evening at the end of July 1974, on my friend's birthday, we decided to go to The Lemon Tree, a disco and gambling casino. It was here that I was to meet my future husband, Neville. Talking as we left the dance floor he told me he was in printing and I found him very interesting. We decided to meet up again. Reflecting back I felt I had known him all my life. We got along so well that on 17 September 1977 we were married, and moved to our new home not far from my mother in Blackpool.

Almost a year later on the 13 June 1978, whilst watching the Granada Television production of 'Will Shakespeare', I had an extraordinary experience. It came to the part of the supposed death of Christopher Marlowe, poet and playwright; at this point I turned to my husband Neville and said, "I didn't die like that!", which you will discover when you read on further. In 1980 on the 15 June our son was born, and we seemed to be compelled to name him Christopher.

My life changed when my husband's company decided to relocate him from Blackpool to Dunstable, Bedfordshire. On 12 February 1981 we moved 'lock, stock and barrel' to Bedfordshire and the Marlowe connection became stronger.

I will begin to explain the reasons behind the outburst "I didn't die like that!" and how this was to affect my life so profoundly from that time on. It was a summer's evening in 1978, my husband, Neville, and myself had decided to sit down and watch 'Will Shakespeare' on television, starring Tim Currie and Ian McShane. We were relaxed and the programme was well underway when it came to the death of a man called Christopher Marlowe. As a dagger was plunged into his eye I turned to Neville exclaiming, "I didn't die like that!"

"Don't you mean, 'He didn't die like that?' "

"No, I know that I mean 'I'. I can't explain why I said it. Those are the words that came out."

We retired to bed, but I tossed and turned unable to get this man, Christopher Marlowe, from my mind.

At breakfast the next morning Neville sensed my unease. "If you feel so passionately about what you have seen why not go to the library and research Marlowe's life?"

It was this suggestion that spurred me to visit the library that evening after work. Enthusiastically I asked the librarian for assistance and found a book called 'Kind Kit' by Hugh Ross Williamson. Once home I soon found myself engrossed in the book, 'an informal biography'. As I became immersed in the story I began to experience flashbacks, as if reliving the life of this man. Yet many of the incidents playing before my eyes were contrary to my reading. Every detail, each event, was so vividly portrayed, as if a film was running on a cinematic screen before my eyes. Reading on I was soon to learn of Marlowe working as a secret agent in Rheims, France. As my gaze misted I felt the sensation of being transported back in time, seeing before me myself as a young Marlowe, dressed in robes of the Catholic ministry, attending a seminary. I experienced an inner sense of fear and anxiety as if I was Marlowe on one of his first missions.

As Brenda Harwood I knew little about this period in history, thinking secret agents to be a modern-day development in the world of espionage, James Bond and all that.

Feeling unnerved by the evening's experiences I sought refuge in a relaxing bath. Here I was, Mrs Ordinary. Until the previous day I had never heard of Christopher Marlowe. Everyone knows about William Shakespeare; I had studied his work at school and liked it, but I had never heard mention of Christopher Marlowe. So who was he and why was he having such an impact on me?

Returning to the book later that evening I read about Marlowe's death at Deptford, London, but felt frustrated and enraged at the inaccuracy of it and hurled the book against the wall. Fortunately it survived intact to be returned to the library, yet I was troubled by the book's contents.

Speaking with a friend regarding the matter she jokingly replied, "Maybe you were there in that time!" Then changing her demeanour she continued seriously, "I'm sure that we come back again, but we are not supposed to believe such things." She had a Catholic background and had been brought up not to believe in reincarnation, yet had an inner feeling that rebirth was the case, although afraid to express it openly.

I replied, "Well whatever it is, I am going to get to the bottom of it." My nature has always been to find out the truth.

Apart from my husband, and briefly my friend, I did not discuss the Marlowe experience with anybody else as something deep within me told me no one would comprehend what I was trying to put across. I myself did not understand what was happening to me. But I knew within my own heart that whatever it was I had experienced I needed to find answers to questions I so wanted to ask. But whom do I ask?

Neville listened patiently and said, "Do more research."

So little appeared to have been written about Christopher Marlowe, but I was able to access a book by A L Rowse, 'Christopher Marlowe: A Biography', which related a similar story to that by Hugh Ross Williamson. However, my attention was arrested by an illustration of a copy of Marlowe's portrait at Corpus Christi College, Cambridge. I sat looking at it for hours, studying the face, drawn by the intensity of the eyes. It was a gaze that appeared far distant, yet on further scrutiny the eyes were full of passion, a passion for what he believed in. 'An old head on young shoulders' came to mind; this was a man old for his years. A slight smile on his lips, arms folded as if to distance himself; yet deep down wanting to be loved, afraid of being hurt. Like myself I thought. I could sense something of this man in myself when a similar age. He had been a rebel and his views not always orthodox, like my own. He was hiding something, what I was not sure, but I needed to know. I decided to keep my impressions to myself and to research when I could. His eyes followed me wherever I went. Christopher Marlowe was here to stay.

I had said that Christopher Marlowe was here to stay and indeed he was. Thoughts of him cascaded through my mind like a tumbling waterfall, as far memories of his life continued to replay in my mind's eye; many of them incidents that to this day have not been recorded. I felt that there was so much that I knew about him. Even when researching I knew what I was going to read.

Dunstable is a small market town steeped in history. The house we moved into was modern, but I always felt, when Neville was out, that I was never alone. When we had first viewed the property Neville had seen a young woman standing by the upper bedroom window, but the estate agent had assured us that the house had been vacant for several months.

We settled down to our new life, Neville enjoying his work at Waterlow's while I stayed housewife and mother. When I was in Dunstable town I experienced an overwhelming feeling of familiarity. It was as if I knew the town, but I had not visited it prior to our move. Although unrecorded I wondered whether Marlowe had had a connection with the town. The Marlowe Society was unable to help when I enquired, but I was convinced that a connection did indeed exist. Sensing a link I determined to record any further far memories.

My family commitments kept me happily occupied. When Christopher was two years old we went, as a family, to [1]Scadbury Manor, Kent, on a day trip organised by the Marlowe Society. The estate had been the home of Sir Thomas Walsingham, a patron of Marlowe. Viewing the manor and grounds, as with Dunstable town, I felt the same intrinsic sense of familiarity, an inner knowing that I had been there before. But strangest of all, Neville, who had had minimal involvement in my Marlowe

---

[1] Scadbury is modern-day name for the place where Thomas Walsingham lived in the 16th century that is referred to later in the book's text as Scathebury.

interest, displayed an unaccountable knowledge of the estate. Scadbury Manor obviously held many secrets for us both.

We were invited to visit again. Subsequently returning and standing in the ruins of the old hall I distinctly heard the bitter weeping of a man. I was profoundly affected by the experience that had not been shared by either Neville or Christopher, yet the crying came again and on this occasion was heard by all.

A friend joined me on a return visit to Scadbury Manor and while there we met with a group of people who, like myself, were researching Christopher Marlowe. They were studying Marlowe from an esoteric angle and as we engaged in conversation they referred to Marlowe's involvement in the School of Night and his profound interest in spiritual awareness. In all innocence I acknowledged this, sensing that I was speaking for Marlowe. However, I mentioned my membership of the Marlowe Society that inadvertently resulted in a communication from its Chairman chiding me for involving myself with the interests of such people. He maintained that their underlying interest stemmed from a curiosity regarding the 'dark arts'. But knowing what I do now I am confident that he himself had scant understanding of such and was misinformed in his assumptions. In due course I was told that my membership of the Society would be withdrawn based upon my misconduct. I considered such action to be retributive and enquired as to whether he had studied Marlowe's 'Doctor Faustus' for surely he must have had esoteric knowledge to write such a play. His reply was that the Society preferred to play down that side of Marlowe's life. In conclusion we agreed to disagree.

It was a year later that I received a call from the Chairman who, having given thought to our conversation, asked me if I would forward him my theories for his personal interest, but stating that they would not go into the Society's archives and thus the public arena. In consequence he introduced me to an American gentleman who explained that he had written a book about Christopher Marlowe expounding his theory that Marlowe had survived his supposed death at Deptford. I was later to meet him when he stayed with Neville and I on his return journey to Canterbury. I found him sincere in his opinions concerning Marlowe and subsequently read his book in which he theorised that it was Christopher Marlowe who had written the works of William Shakespeare as similarities of style exist between the plays of both. I respected his views and outlined my experiences, but although interested he was looking for material evidence to support his theories. He suggested I seek professional advice from a reputable psychic as he felt this could be my pathway, although not his. I pondered his advice and, on the suggestion of a colleague of Neville's, contacted the secretary of the local Spiritualist Church who put us in touch with a respected medium in the area. It was with his skills and advice that I was to begin to understand the phenomenon affecting my life. I was starting to talk in the first person and in a different accent and manner.

Shortly after visiting the medium both Neville and I attended a Psychic Supper at a local Spiritualist Church. It was there that we met Ernie White. During our conversation with him he suggested that he could give me crystal healing to help with my eye disability.

While he gave me crystal healing Ernie discovered that several of my chakras (energy centres) were out of balance and blocked. Although I was not familiar with this technique, Ernie reassuringly explained that he felt confident it would assist in establishing the root cause of my experiences. He conducted a further session using crystals and meditation, I felt myself change has I had before, then I stated my name as Christopher Marley, which had been the accepted spelling of Marlowe at that time, and further added that I was living in

France. He asked the month and I replied that it was October, thereby establishing the fact that Marlowe had been alive in the latter part of 1593 and had not died in May of that year as recorded. I sat up and had an interesting conversation with him.

On looking back at some of my earlier writing I came across a scribbled: 'France, November 1593,' and so began another episode in the unravelling of the Marlowe connection.

The visions began again and when recounting them I automatically spoke in the first person as before. When quietly meditating I would change imperceptibly, my mannerisms becoming more defined, my voice becoming deeper and gently accented when addressing Neville. I would become another character, conversing on subjects regarding spiritual matters and esoteric knowledge with a passion and awareness that was not my own. When Ernie, his wife and friends joined us for circle meetings I would unaccountably become this now familiar 'other person', ready to hold discourse and intellectualise on all manner of subjects about which I personally had little knowledge. More and more I was relaxing into the persona of Christopher Marlowe. I had no control over what was happening to me and Ernie kindly advised Neville on how to deal with me under these circumstances. Yet as this phenomenon continued to occur the clairvoyant side of me began to develop noticeably.

It was one evening, as I was sitting in the bedroom, I felt myself become absorbed. I was aware of the gradual sensation of my features changing, I felt the facial hair of beard and moustache, my body feeling distinctly male. I was wearing a brown woollen doublet and hose together with knee length riding boots, a cloak clasped about my shoulders. I was mounted on horseback, my hands resting upon the pommel. Suddenly I spurred my steed to a canter across a field, the echo of hoof beats drumming beneath me, cloak caught by the wind; stopping momentarily to cast my gaze around me in agitation. Then tears began to well up in my eyes, my heart was heavy, a feeling of sadness in my breast. I must leave those I held so dear. With gloved hand I wiped the tears from my eyes. Then I spurred my mount faster across the field as if in haste. I would take ship to France and there wait for instruction. Riding, feeling so unhappy, thinking what a fool I had been, caught in a web of deceit. Now I must leave my home forever, never to return… Then the vision went, drifting into the mists of time. It left me feeling so strange; I couldn't get it out of my mind. I felt such sadness, a sense of loss. I felt the impulse to write and my words took the form of a poem. As I wrote rain began to fall and I felt it had been doing the same in that century, for the rain represented the tears I had been crying, and that many had been shed in that lifetime. My heart had been shattered into so many fragments.

As the poem neared completion I felt a compulsion to tell his story, that the life of Christopher Marlowe must be recorded as I knew it, regardless of public opinion. It was as if I had carried this for so long in my spirit. For centuries it had sought acknowledgement, calling out to be heard, and now was the time to tell. Yet Neville was concerned that people might not understand, that they were not ready for what I had to tell, and that ridicule would follow in its wake. My reply was simple, "I don't care what people think, it's not about me personally, and it's about the pain a man has been carrying with him for over 400 years." And I started to document memories whenever I could.

Returning home from shopping one day in 1999? I turned on the television in time to see 'Good Morning' on ITV 1. Most interestingly a man by the name of Tom Barlow was being interviewed about his work as a psychotherapist with reference to a lady called A J Stewart. She apparently had a far-memory of being James IV of Scotland, the onset of which had began when she was 16 years old, and resulted in her books

'Falcon: The autobiography of His Grace James IV the King of Scots' and 'King's Memory: An Autobiography.' Listening to the interview I felt as if Spirit had heard my cries at last. As the programme ended I noted the Helpline number and rang immediately. I was kindly given Tom Barlow's personal telephone number and contacted him, briefly outlining what had been happening to me, and at his request forwarding a summary. Tom had researched far-memory experiences and, having read my synopsis, phoned to offer his support. I felt so confident speaking to Tom, learning that I was not alone in my experiences and that there were others out there going through the same experiences as myself. It was a comforting thought to at last know that I was not going mad.

It was also reassuring to know that not only did I have Neville's continuing support, but also that I now had a friend and advisor in Tom Barlow. He kept in touch with me on a regular basis, giving me the strength to continue recording my experiences and trying to formulate a book. People volunteered to help me in this venture, but due to other commitments or an inability to empathise with the character of Marlowe, they abandoned the project and I found myself unable to make positive progress. I so wanted to start my book, to speak for Christopher Marlowe, but the time did not seem to be right. I would have to be patient. The time would come, but it was not yet.

Tom expressed interest in meeting me and I likewise. In the meantime he suggested I read A J Stewart's books. Enthusiastically I ordered them and eagerly awaited their arrival. Once I began to read firstly 'Falcon: The Autobiography of His Grace James IV, King of Scots', followed by 'King's Memory: An Autobiography' of A J Stewart, I was intrigued. I was able to identify with the experiences presented by A J Stewart who herself had a far-memory experience. It was consoling to know that she too had been so deeply affected by memories impacting on her 20th century reality. Yet again

I felt myself inspired to continue writing, confident in the knowledge that I was not one alone in my truth, but that where there was one like me there would be others.

Tom contacted me a few months later asking whether I would be interested in appearing on 'Granada Breeze', one of the Sky networks. He himself was to be on the programme together with another past-life regressionist, Judy Hall. The programme was scheduled for 14 February at Granada Studios, Manchester. I readily accepted with Neville, my son, Christopher and a friend, happy to join me in what I hoped would prove to be a positive platform for far-memory.

Tom was also keen for me to participate in an introductory interview at my home the week before filming at the studio. I agreed and the camera crew duly arrived, albeit an hour late, having been unable to find our home. After tea and sandwiches the crew began to set up their equipment. All was going well, but we realised the microphone wasn't picking up my voice. The crew tried three battery power packs, all to no avail. It wasn't until Neville suggested removing some of his crystals from the room that we realised the current of power had been interrupted by the energy of the crystals. Things finally got underway.

The interviewer was a pleasant person, patient and understanding, and interested in the subject she was filming. She asked about my far-memory and how it had led me to Tom Barlow; and it proved to be a successful evening. It boded well for the main interview a week later.

Our invited group travelled to Manchester where we were met and warmly greeted by Tom. I found him a really genuine person, very straightforward, an earnest Scotsman. We were introduced to Judy Hall and the interviewer; then I was shown to a room to change my outfit prior to filming. However when I presented myself for interview there was obvious disappointment on the part of the interviewer who expected me to be donned in the garb of Marlowe's period. My frank reply was, "I am a 20th Century Elizabethan and I am now Brenda Harwood, not Christopher Marlowe. I only have the far-memory of Marlowe and what would I gain by dressing like him? Doing that would ruin the whole validity of what I am trying to put across to the public." She seemed rather put out by this, but Tom admired me for what I had said. And this in turn endeared him to me.

Filming got underway, but Tom was disappointed that although I was briefly shown being interviewed I was not invited to sit with Judy Hall or him; and that for much of the programme I was obscured from view by the interviewer, allowing me little opportunity to speak. However Tom and Judy were able to state their case and spoke with quiet confidence, while their views were vociferously challenged by a scientist who considered me to be on an 'ego trip'. Taking exception to his attitude I countered his opinions when attending the after filming buffet. I commented that if I was, as he claimed, on an 'ego trip' then why was I going through so much emotional trauma? Choosing not to look me in the eye he said that he was unable to scientifically explain such a phenomenon. I felt this to be inconclusive and insubstantial, and was heartened to see that Science does not hold all the answers.

We bid our farewells to Tom and his friend, Margaret. He thanked me for coming, saying that he was looking forward to doing more work with me, and stressed that I must not be discouraged by negative views. I replied that I was not worried about opposition for, in controversial matters such as mine, one would always meet with those for or against. And over the years I had developed a skin like a rhino. Thanking him I said how much he had helped change my life, in that I was now more positive and able to embark on my quest of following through in writing what is my truth.

So now I begin to tell my truth to you of my far-memory of the poet and playwright, and secret agent, Christopher Marlowe.

This book has been written primarily to help other's who have been experiencing the same as I have for the last twenty eight years. I hope when they read this book they will know that they are not alone and I am here to empathise with what they are going through.

Chapter 1

My home life and schooldays in Canterbury

I was born on a Wednesday, 23 February in the year of our Lord, 1564 in Canterbury on a winter's morn. On the 26 February I was carried over to the church of St George and baptised as Christopher Marlowe where I was named after both of my grandparents. My father was John Marlowe a shoemaker, tanner and guildsman and my mother, whose maiden name was Katherine Arthur, was the daughter of a clergyman from Dover. I was my parent's second child, the oldest being my sister Mary, who was two year's older than me.

I grew up in George Street, at a shoemaker's shop, which had three levels to it. The ground floor of the shop had shutters at the front that jutted out onto the street. The bottom shutter was used as a counter for serving goods and there were hooks at the top where father kept one boot and one shoe in various styles, for both adults and children. He hung samples of tooled leather that showed different styles and patterns. To the left side of the shutters was a door, so customers were able to come into the shop.

At the back of the shop was a room and workshop where my father and his three apprentices worked. A large wooden bench was fixed along one side; it had shelves above for the lasts and tools. On the other side was another row of shelves, holding the cured hides. From this room a door led out to the kitchen, it had a cooking range with cooking pots, on hooks, hanging above the fire. These were never empty, as mother always had vegetables and whatever meat that was left over from the roast. In the middle of the room was a large wooden table with a bench either side or a chair at each end for mother and father. In another corner was a bench for preparing food, which had shelves above for storage and at the side were two cupboards. At the far end of the kitchen was the cellar door which mother always kept locked, and to the right of it was a door leading out to the tannery yard at the back of the shop.

Father would tan and cure the leather at the back in his tanning shed, for making shoes, belts and other leather goods. You could imagine, in high summer weather, the tannery yard wouldn't smell very pleasant, especially in the shed where he hung his hides. On the other side of the shed he kept a barrel of urine which he used for softening the hides and I can remember when I was young, father lifted me up to piss in the barrel.

In the corner of the kitchen was a staircase leading up to the main living quarters and spacious parlour. There was a welcoming fireplace with a hearth and wooden mantle above, on which stood two iron candlesticks. The room had wainscoting made of light oak. Facing the parlour door was a window that opened out onto the main street. In front of it was a table that had a chair at each side and a wooden bowl of fruit and nuts. Beside the fireplace stood a settle with beautiful embroidered cushions that mother made and beside it was a chest where mother kept her sewing needles and threads. Opposite the fireplace was a large sideboard where mother kept her best pots and cloths and on it were two wooden candlesticks with the family bible resting in the centre, father's pride possession, at the other end was a wooden bowl filled to the brim with pot-pourri, its scent filled the room. On the wall at side of the fireplace were shelves with a few bottles of homemade wine, tankards and cups. Scattered about the room were small wooden stools for us children to sit on, and there was a wooden box where we kept our toys. Mother always kept them in there, so we could play inside during the winter months or bad weather. Across the hall was another room that became my bedchamber, which had a small window that looked out over the tannery yard. The wainscoting in my bedchamber was made of pine and I had the 'second best' bed as it was called with azure blue curtains around, a matching coverlet on the bed, linen sheets, woollen blankets, a feather mattress and bolster. There was a fireplace opposite the bed with a candlestick on the mantle, and beside it was a small table with pitcher and bowl.

The table and chair at the side of the window had on it a wooden candlestick and in the corner of the room was a chest where I kept my clothes, mother sprinkled them with lavender, to keep them fresh. She said that it helped them smell sweet and it kept away the fleas. I enjoyed having a bedchamber to myself away from my sisters, as they often wet their bed and were always fighting. There were two large bedchambers on the top floor of the house, the front being mother's and father's and at the back slept my sisters in truckle beds with two chests for their clothes, and a table in the window with two pitchers and a bowl.

Our house and shop was always busy, the family hustling and bustling around. I often helped father clean the hides in the tannery and served in the shop on the Saturday afternoons, and on quiet days he showed me how to tool leather.

My mother had nine children but not all survived, the boys were the weakest and I had four other sisters, Margaret, Joan, Anne and Dorothy, all younger than Mary and myself. I had only two brothers who were both called Thomas, but sadly didn't survive. I had another brother, who survived, whose arrival was abrupt, and he too was called Thomas. Methinks mother was determined to have a son named after her brother, Thomas Arthur. He was born in 1576, when I was almost twelve years old, I remember the birth well, our maid was out at the market when my mother's water broke, so father went out to look for her. Mother couldn't climb the stairs to her bedchamber as the pains kept coming quickly. She told me to scatter cushions off the settle on the floor for her to lie on and it was there she gave birth to my one only surviving brother. I helped mother with the birth as she told me what to do, and after I went upstairs to the bedchamber for a blanket to wrap my brother in. Mother insisted that he was baptised straight away because she was worried that the fairies would come and steal him and leave a changeling in his place. Unfortunately I didn't see much of Thomas as he was growing up, for I left home for university when he was only four years old.

I recall my sister Mary dying when I was about four years old, a sad time for the family. She ran out into the street, and not looking where she was going, fell and hit her head on the cobbles at the back of the house. My father carried her upstairs to the parlour and laid her on the settle at the side of the fire, her head was covered in blood but alas she wasn't moving. Mother tried frantically to revive her, but to no avail. This was the first time I saw mother and father weep. I remember running up the stairs screaming, I knew even at this early age, my sister Mary had died.

There were to be many tragedies in my life, but having to experience the death of Mary, who I loved dearly, why was it she had to die so young? To this day I can see her face, she was like an angel with a mop of red, golden curls and pale blue eyes and the fairest of complexion I have ever seen. She always looked after me, dressed me, brushed my hair and held my hand tightly when we went out walking together.

Mother and father were heartbroken, as she was their first-born and mother kept her amber necklace as a keepsake, to remember her by.

Margaret, my other sister was a year younger than me and I kept her close after Mary's death, as I was frightened I might lose her too. Though she was a bit of a shrew she became my favourite sister, we got on together well, but she vexed me at times, as she was lazy.

One-day mother was out at the market and told Margaret to do her chores. She laid in bed, lazy madam which made me angry, so I went into her bedchamber and pulled her out the bed by her hair and made her do the chores. I wouldn't have done this, but she really got me vexed, for mother had told me to make sure she did what she was asked.

As a child I suffered with poor health and spent a lot of time in bed with a chesty cough. Mother was concerned it could have been consumption, but she nursed me back to good health and through time I became stronger, after this mother and I grew closer. One day in conversation mother mentioned that father said I looked like her, but she said may be so, but you have your father's temper and arrogance, and that she said you will have to curb, for it could get you into trouble one day. I always enjoyed talking to her, unlike father she was unable to read, but she had much knowledge of herbs and was nimble with her fingers making lace, sewing and embroidery. She was patient and understanding, kind and good-hearted and always there to help people less fortunate than herself. Even when she was busy around the house she would stop and listen to what we had to say and often she would sit down with me in the evening and talk when father had gone out to the inn and my sisters had retired to bed. When we were talking she always had something in her hands, if it wasn't sewing or making lace, she would embroider the collars and cuffs of our shirts and petticoats for the girls. I helped mother prepare the pot-pourri to scent all the rooms and our clothes, and I would collect acorn cups to add for decoration. The pot-pourri included lavender, which I was very fond of.

When I was young, mother would curl my hair and said I was too pretty to be a boy as I had a fair complexion that I kept until later in life. She gave me a cross that was my grandsire's and a pendant set in amber to protect me from evil. Mother always said I was destined for the church, for she promised God that her first son would be his servant. This angered father at times because he wanted me to carry on the family trade. As time went on and my brother was born, father realised he could train Thomas to carry on the family trade and started to appreciate that I had talents far beyond that of a shoemaker. When he wasn't working he and Uncle Thomas, mother's brother, helped me with my reading, using stories from the scriptures in the family bible. On Sunday the family would attend service at St George's Church, across the road from the shop and in the evening we would sit in the parlour where father would ask me to read a passage from the family Bible.

Father and I would go fishing at a river not far away from our home, a treat for me, as he was always busy. He was a strict man, but fair and he always insisted that we all should help mother around the house. I had the job of chopping wood and kindling for the fire, put it into baskets and carried them upstairs to the parlour and bedchambers. I had to polish the wainscoting on the walls of my bedchamber. What used to vex me was when I was given extra chores my lazy sister Margaret should have done for mother. As Margaret was father's favourite, he would often let her stay in bed, allowing her to get away with it, but I thought this was unfair, but if we spoke ill of her, father would chide us all and we were sent to bed without supper.

My Truth

When I was sent to bed early I would often climb out of my bedchamber window and sit on top of the shed in the tannery yard at the back of the house. Sometimes Meg (our cat) and I sat together and gazed at the moon. Lucky for me, father never caught me doing this, for if he had done; I would have got a good hiding.

From the age of seven or eight I liked to spend a lot of time on my own, going for a walk around the ruins at St Augustine's Abbey. I spent many a time there deep in thought and went for a walk in the woods by the river where father and I went fishing. Nature and all its beauty held a deep fascination for me. It was at this place one evening in 1577 a terrible thing happened. I was robbed of my innocence, but I will speak of this later. I have always felt at one with nature, for I believed that there were elementals in the woods that tended the flowers and trees and were part of the great mystery of life. I must confess as a child I was a day-dreamer, something mother would often chide me for, especially at the dinner table, instead of eating my food I would drift off in my mind to a wood or river, for I believed water had healing powers. Deep in thought with my mind wondering, I would suddenly drop my spoon, then mother would say: "Christopher ..." are you day-dreaming again. I had a fascination with the moon, when darkness fell I would gaze at it from my bedchamber window and be in awe of it's magic. I believed that the moon controlled nature and its cycle and I wrote many a verse down that would spring to my mind.

I would write small verses on scraps of paper, if I there were any to spare, and read them to my sister Margaret. I had a box that belonged to my grandsire (my father's father) in which I kept these verses, keepsakes and treasures that I collected on my walks by the river and woods. I kept this box throughout my life, in Cambridge, London, Scadbury and my exile in Padua.

Brenda Harwood

I was a sensitive child, and a dreamer who felt trapped, even as a young boy and I didn't fit in with my parents' way of thinking or with the family. In some respects I was alone, it wasn't because I didn't love them, quite the opposite, I just felt they didn't understand me, so I didn't feel part of them. All I wanted to do was write verse and gain knowledge, for I would often imagine myself walking in ancient Greece or feeling that I am on the mighty Acropolis. Something I was never able to realise or experience, only in my dream state, I would be surrounded by all the famous Greek philosophers and poets and wanted so much to write poetry and plays about great conquerors, kings and magic.

The thoughts of magic were with me at an early age, for me magic was real; it was all around us even in everyday life. Later when I was much older I learned about the people I dreamed of. Uncle Thomas had two wonderful books about Greek philosophers that belonged to my grandsire on my mother's side and father had a book about King Arthur. Uncle Thomas would discuss his books with me and he shared his own beliefs and philosophy.

I spent many hours alone in my bedchamber quietly meditating, asking the question, why me, why am I drawn to this path, but I was never given an answer, only that you know the answer, for it lies within you. I believe if you want to achieve a goal you must focus your thoughts on achieving it, then and only then will it happen for you. It is more important that you accept what is given to you. In many of my discussions with Uncle Thomas and father they believed this too. Father told me that he wanted to be a master shoemaker and he achieved it.

When I was about nine years old my dear friend William died in a fire. A lighted candle fell over on a table at side of a window in his bedchamber. Unfortunately he was trapped and his parents were unable to get to him. So he was burnt alive. I saw the flames and could hear him scream that day. After this I often heard his screams in my mind in a dream state. He told me not to punish myself because I wasn't able to save him. Your father did what he thought was right. He held you back from going into the house to save me because he loved you and feared for your safety. His tortured cries lay within me for many years afterwards. This was a great sadness and that tragedy. From this time onwards, I was always wary of candles and frightened of fire.

In later years all the memories of this tragic death came flooding back to me when I saw people being burnt at the stake. Something that I was fearful of myself especially when I was in danger of being condemned by the State. To me, it is a terrible thing, for when you are burnt there is nothing left of you except a pile of ashes. I remember the church saying if you burnt in a fire you would go to hell. This to me was nonsense.

It was after this point in my life I started to get bad headaches and suffer attacks of rage. I used to have loss of memory during these attacks. I recall seeing William the day before he died but a strange thing happened. When he turned and said goodbye I turned round for a split second and I saw him as a charred skeleton. It was awful for I couldn't understand why I had this vision of him in this way. Of course I realised after the fire, why. This was the first of many visions I was later to experience. While growing up I always believed I was different to others in my family and friends, so this incident proved this to me.

When I was ten years old we had to leave our home in George Street. Father owed too much money so we couldn't afford to pay the rent. I loved our home so much, in truth; I felt a great loss and sadness, so much so I was unable to settle into any other place. For me that felt like a home and I never forgave father for losing it, neither did mother. There was a strong attachment to the house. I had my own chamber with pine wainscoting; it was a sanctuary to me. Father tried to make amends by saying that I would have a room of my own in the new house, but I said it wasn't the same.

The most humiliating part of the move was pushing the handcart by moonlight down the cobbled back streets of Canterbury with our belongings and one of my sisters sitting on it. Father thought it best we move out during night-time. You can imagine us can't you, all of us trundling over the cobblestones and the cart wheels clattering. All our worldly possessions on top, stealing away silently like thieves in the night.

I never did settle in the new home although mother tried her best to make us feel comfortable. As we were short of money for a while she embroidered tablecloths and made fine lace to raise money for us. This helped to feed and clothe us and pay for a maid, Marian, to come in and help care for us and help mother with the housework. Of course mother kept this money away from father for if he'd got his hands on it he'd spend it foolishly. Mother said the reason father never made much money was because he would mend shoes and take goods for his work, such as eggs, beef, mutton or cloth. He wasn't a good businessman, lackadaisical in asking for money owed to him. I remember them both rowing over this. She complained that bartering for goods didn't pay the bills. In the evening he would go to the inn to drink and wager and fall asleep on the settle by the fire when he came back. What money we had mother hid, for if father were given the chance, he would gamble it away on foolish wagers. Mother said he would bet on two fleas running on a dog's back for the sake of a wager.

I think we would have had more money had father not gambled or got himself into debt. I didn't like to think of these times, as this part of my life was too distressing. I lost track of times father was in lawsuits. He was forever suing others for non-payment of bills and because of this put himself in debt and placed his family in jeopardy. It caused many rows and arguments between mother and him.

Let me tell you a little more about my father. He was a fine figure of man with a fresh, ruddy complexion and had sandy-red coloured hair that receded at the front. He had a moustache and no beard. He stood 5 feet 8 inches in height, but had a paunch due to his heavy drinking, as he liked his ale. Oftimes he was abrupt with Mother, especially when he wanted his dinner. He'd say to Mother: "where's my dinner woman". He did this one-day and ended up wearing it. "That'll teach you John for talking to me in that way." Father was very pig-headed, he was right and everybody else was wrong. Oft times when he was drunk he would be very obliging, a gossip-mongerer, but he would not pass the gossip on, instead he would use it for his own ends. Mother often said he was too nosy for his own good and it would get him into trouble one day. One night she lost her temper completely and threw several bottles of preserve at him. She threatened to leave him and said she would go and live with my uncle. Father promised faithfully on his bended knees he would mend his ways. If mother was angry she could be a shrew, a trait Margaret took after. Many years later when I wrote 'The Taming of the Shrew' I had my mother and sister in mind when writing the part of Katherine.

Mother bore nine children, six survived, four girls and two boys. She was a comely woman in later years and had a fair complexion with some freckles scattered around her nose, which annoyed her at times. She would dab them with vinegar, hoping to try and dispel them. She became rather rounded in later years but kept her curves and even kept her long flaxen tresses, which reached, to her waist, which she wore in plaits. The last time I saw she had not one grey hair on her head. Generally she would wear brown and grey dresses with a shift underneath made of a creamy-white material, but she had two best dresses, one was blue and the other was black for sombre occasions. She liked jewellery and always wore a posy ring given to her by my father. She was a good cook and kept a good house, but believed in keeping her own counsel and was angry about father's openness, as he was always getting into verbal disputes. I suppose this is why she hated his behaviour at times. The house was never dirty; floors were cleaned and scrubbed every day. A fastidious person dedicated to her home and family and always held the family together. We had good wholesome food, such as stews, and there was always a potage going on the fire. Mother taught the girls to sew and embroider; two of my sisters who followed in her footsteps were Joan and Margaret. The other two, Anne and Dorothy were sows, for mother used to spoil them; they looked like butter wouldn't melt in their mouths. I got really cross with Dorothy one day because she used to pinch my flesh, particularly my arms as she went passed me and other times she would do it at the dinner table. I remember her grabbing my arm and deliberately twisting the flesh.

Many things happened to me around the age of ten strangely enough. I helped out in a local inn as a potboy, collecting pots and cleaning, which helped bring in extra coppers for the family. While working there I saw a young girl being raped by the innkeeper. His name escapes me, but I remember mother being very angry that I was a witness to such a thing. I was going down into the cellar to collect some bottles and innkeeper was there too. A young girl came down the stairs for something; I can't remember what it was exactly. Just at that moment the innkeeper grabbed her by the arm and she screamed out; leave me alone! The innkeeper wasn't aware I was looking. At first I didn't know what was going on. I got afraid so hid out of the way still in view of what was happening. It was terrible what he was doing to her. He had undone her garments and she was crying. I recall her running passed me

My Truth

saying she had been raped. I ran home immediately and told mother what I had seen and heard.

The constable was called to the inn and I had to be a witness. My mother told me always to tell the truth, this I did when I spoke to the constable. Afterwards mother told me never to think on it again. The innkeeper was heavily fined and I believe he was flogged for raping the young girl. Needless to say, mother didn't allow me to go back to work at the inn.

I remember the Queen visiting Canterbury when I was about ten years old as well. I was standing at our parlour window in an upper room along with my mother, father and little sisters. We were watching the long procession winding its way through the streets. I looked at one of the courtiers and said to myself, one day I would meet those people and speak to the Queen. For some reason I knew that I wouldn't be spending the rest of life here in Canterbury or follow the trade of my father. I wanted to be a writer even though my mother had high hopes of me becoming a clergyman like her father. I knew the church wasn't for me, but to please mother I went to Corpus Christi College in Cambridge. What happened there I will speak of in detail later. Suffice it to say I was only two weeks away from taking up holy orders, but wasn't able to go through with it.

I discovered later it was Uncle Thomas who also helped to pay towards my education. I was deeply indebted to him and regretted in some way that I didn't enter the church. I couldn't be a hypocrite, even though at times I was a 'divine in show'. So I decided to decline the offer of a parish and refused to be ordained.

I think father realised that I didn't want to go into his trade, so he decided I should have a good education. So it began, first at petty school as it was called and then onto King's School. For me this was the beginning of a long journey, a journey, where I was to seek and learn knowledge, truth and intrigue. For what feeds me, destroys me. *Quod me nutrit, me destruit*, later to become my motto.

I went to petty school as it was called, connected to the Church of St George. I attended the school every day except Saturday, as I helped father in his shop. It was here I learned the basics, reading, writing and arithmetic.

Father wanted me to go onto King's School but he couldn't afford it. So he spoke to the headmaster, Reverend Sweating, who was a friend of John Gressop, the headmaster at King's. He explained to him that I was too advanced for me years and he couldn't teach me anything more. John Gressop agreed to a reduced fee to take me into King's School at the age of 12, but only part-time for two or three days a week.

Before entering King's School full time at 14 years old, I had to sit an exam. I passed and was allowed to go to King's, which pleased my mother and father. I wore a purple gown. My studies were Latin, rhetoric, arithmetic, English languages and literature. I learned some Greek, although I wasn't much good at this subject, history, singing and music. It was always my ambition to translate Latin to English, giving the common man a chance to read. I also believed later on in years, a woman should be allowed to have an education. If a woman had the wit to do so, why not give her the opportunity.

I became a chorister in the cathedral choir. The choirmaster was very proud of me; he said I had a singing voice like an angel. Mother and father were proud too and were honoured that I had been given the opportunity to join the cathedral choir and be a member of such a fine school. I spend many evenings studying and gaining knowledge. I learned Latin and Greek. I remained at King's School until I left and went to Corpus Christi College, Cambridge. Our hours were long and as a chorister I would sing after school. My knowledge of Latin was excellent but I wasn't all that good at Greek.

My Truth

John Gressop, the headmaster, favoured me in many ways. He was a kind man who felt if you were worthy of his help would encourage and nurture your talent. He said I had many qualities that would later make me a fine academic. So I considered it an honour and a privilege for him to allow me access to his private library and look through his books. It gave me the opportunity to be among so much knowledge and learning. He saw that I was learned and wanted to show his kindness. It was he who made me overcome my lack of concentration at times. In class, I often sketched pixies on his essays and down the sides of some of the pages. Having seen what I had scrawled on my essays, he was concerned, for he noticed that I was a daydreamer and wanted to help.

I would describe him as being a slim gentleman, of about 5 feet 6 inches in height. He had a salt-and-pepper hair (brown going on grey), chiselled features with high cheekbones and was clean-shaven. He stood straight and walked with a firm step (for he said he knew when anyone was behind him). He spoke clearly and concisely and his voice showed compassion. Authoritative at times, but he was firm and fair and didn't suffer fools gladly. Always dressed sombrely with a small white ruff around his neck.

There was one thing he was strict on, he never believed in severely punishing you unless it was absolutely necessary. Thankfully, it never came to this for any of the students at the school, or me. He felt, violence bred violence, so by treating a student in this way you weren't able to bring out the best in them.

His library was magnificent; it had many books on a variety of subjects ranging from philosophy that interested me most, religion, the classics, history and hundreds more. In particular he had a copy of Holinshed Chronicles, which chronicled the history of the British Isles. When I was looking through his books I discovered a part of history that has been hidden from me. The books contained famous conquerors like Hannibal and Tamburlaine and many others, whom I wrote about later in my plays. There were books on philosophers such as Plato and his writing about Atlantis. I also enjoyed the works of Socrates, Homer, Virgil and Ovid. From this time onwards I was greatly fascinated by the Greeks. Later I translated many books into English about subjects like the Trojan Wars and Helen of Troy. I wanted to translate classical works so that the common-folk would be able to read it. My schoolmaster John Gressop agreed that this would be a very good idea.

He reprimanded me on several occasions for running about in the school corridors and for being late. He realised that something wasn't right. I started to behave like this shortly after the time I was raped. He could see the changes in me, changes uncharacteristic of my usual behaviour. My studies were suffering and he recognised this. He noticed that I began to 'go into myself' and I became unruly. I could see this was upsetting for him, so I tried to change my ways.

He allowed me to borrow his own private books and he gave me a signed copy of Ovid's poetry, Ovid's Elegies and The Amores, which I treasured all my life. As time went by I was asked to help those who were not able to learn as quickly as me, I got them involved in drama, acting, choreography and costumes. Owing to my beauty I generally took the girl's parts. I was not a bounder at King's School, contrary to others beliefs. The days were long; they started at seven in the morning until seven in the evening. Each day we had to be up and out of our beds, washed and changed into our gowns of episcopal purple and ready for matins. Once we had finished we would break our fast before the lessons of the day started. Dinner was in the refectory from one of the clock until two.

Towards the latter end of my time at King's School I became a prefect. I was always scholarly looking at life in a philosophical way.

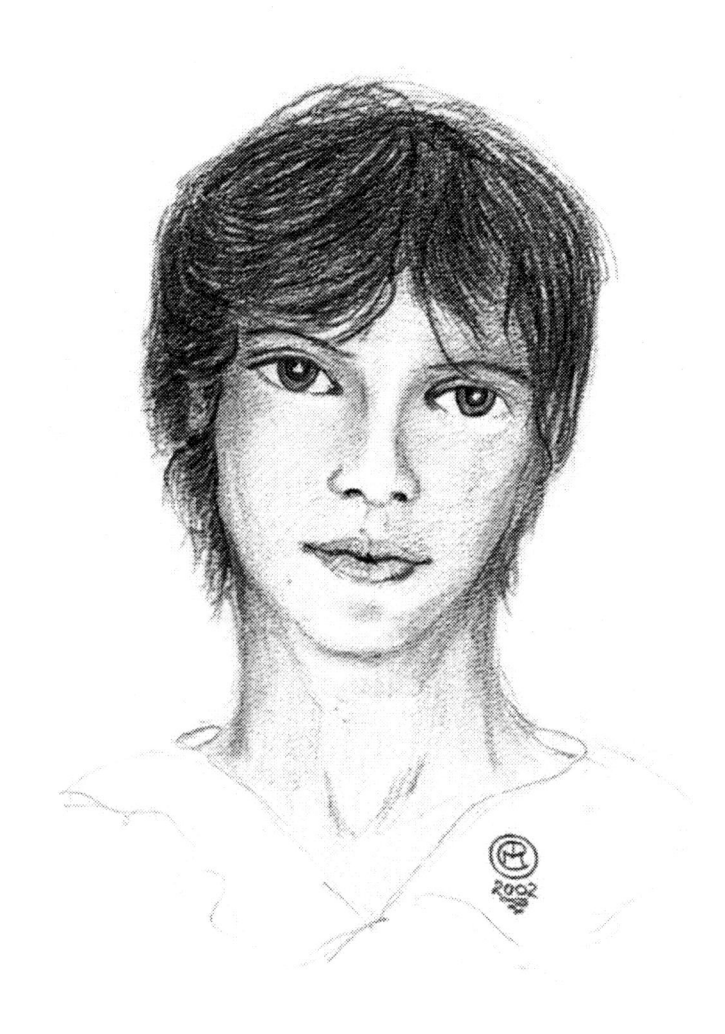

Christopher Marlowe as a boy by psychic
artist David Calvert-Orange

Chapter 2

University years

I passed, on the second time, a scholarship set by Archbishop Parker, entered Benet's College, later to be called Corpus Christi, Cambridge in late December 1579 and in all stayed there for just over six years. It was not until the New Year that I was due to commence my studies and having arrived early for the new term, I shared a dormitory. With me I brought a box packed with food and preserves that my mother had prepared. My three fellow students and I shared our victuals and had a feast. Our attire was plain, like that of a monk and we were told that our hair must either be cut short or tied back. It was so cold in the winter months that it was difficult to think or write, for we were only allowed so much wood for the fire.

When I entered the university my mind was set on becoming a country parson, to take my Bachelor of Arts and then my Master of Arts, like all the other Parker students. I was allowed a small stipend for each year. I struck up a friendship with my room-mate, Thomas Luger, we would discuss philosophical debates and sometimes argue, they were not angry exchanges, more in the way of sensible debate and not long after this we would be supping ale together at the Eagle Inn across the way from the college.

Brenda Harwood

There was a magnificent library there, where I would spend many hours perusing the volumes and making notes for writing poetry and plays. (Some of the rare books were on chains so they could not be removed from the library by the students.) It was there that I first started to write seriously, for it helped me to keep my sanity, as there were times I needed to escape from reality and my writing allowed me to do that, entering a world of fantasy and make-belief. In many of the plays there would be a character that mirrored my own. There was also a poem I wrote called 'Corinna', that shocked those who read it, but my thoughts were upon a boy in a woman's place. After getting my Bachelor of Arts degree and Master of Arts degree, I would be obligated to be ordained into the church and take Holy Orders. If I had done this I would have been the Reverend Christopher Marlowe – not really me at all.

I studied the scriptures and classics: Erasmus's New Testament; Homer's Elegies; Virgil; Plato; Aristotle; Socrates; Ovid; Latin and Greek. We would read and discuss the scriptures and various other religion's views, rhetoric, writing of sermons and translating from one language to another. I was also in the university choir, which was obligatory on entry, and would occasionally write music, study the Arts and learn to draw and paint. Mathematics, which I found boring, was also part of our studies. It was Greek philosophy that intrigued me the most. My mind was set on translating Greek and Roman works into English, especially for those less fortunate in their understanding to be able to read. Therefore took it upon myself to translate Lucan's First Book and, in later years, Ovid's Elegies and various other works. My tutor through these years was Thomas Harris, MA. We would have long discussions with him about the Old and New Testaments and often questioned the belief that Christianity was the oldest religion. Yet before that there had been paganism, and in

My Truth

looking at pagan beliefs and Christianity there was a parallel, as pre-Christian beliefs were one of the same.

I realise that many people were shocked by my statements when I spoke of Jesus and his disciples, but I could not see God sitting there in judgment, instead saw him as an energy and a living force. I stated that Jesus was in love with one of his disciples and that three of them were of my persuasion, but I did not say these things in anger, or meant to be in any way blasphemous. Maybe I was careless in my views and should perhaps have kept them to myself because man was not yet ready. My views brought me onto the path of paganism, for I always knew that the church festivals were of pagan origin. I remember once listening to my father telling me when we had talks together away from mother. He told me the origin of the Green Man and the reason it was put over the outside door, about the fairy folk and other such legends, things that I knew of and believed. For me the pagan way of life was less ritualised and more able to be understood by all people. When my mind was set I devised a motto for myself: 'Quod me nutrit, me destruit' – 'That which feeds me, destroys me'. I shall explain. As a child I was taught to believe God's word, but as I grew up and discovered the real truth this came to destroy me. For all those years I felt I had been living a lie, but for speaking the truth I was condemned by my fellow scholars. I painted a self-portrait on a wooden panel and gave it to the university on leaving, it had my motto in the background to give a clue to its artist and to those who knew me. I then decided to write a book on my thoughts and opinions of the scriptures, it was printed on the continent, but I believe it was burnt by the Church, along with extracts of it in pamphlets, for they were afraid of the truth. My answer to them was they were 'hypocritical asses' and that the Christian religion was formed to keep man in awe. These holy men stood in their pulpits and pontificated upon the acts of Sodom and Gomorrah, of fornication and the 'seven deadly sins', but what did they do when they took off their robes and came out of the churches? They committed those sins, so to me they were nothing short of hypocrites and in later years I told them to their faces.

I had a fiery temper and could not stand ignorance and hypocrisy; I was many things, but never a hypocrite, as I could not be pleasant for the sake of it. If I did not like someone I told them, for I was not like the Church and the Government who were full of hypocrisy. If I felt someone was a hypocrite I told them. I expected honesty and truth from people and looked for those qualities from my friends, but I did not expect them to love me. What I hated most was people who would be pious in the face of others, while going against the principles they stood for. They were pompous asses, all eating out of the same trough. I felt everyone should have an equal opportunity and people should be treated in a better manner than they were. There was such ignorance, and people died unnecessarily. Hated the way the Church kept people in fear and refused to wear a cross, even though I had a cross which belonged to one of my grandsires. Rather than destroy it, I gave it to my dear sister Margaret who I loved so much. The cross was used to persecute... people were so afraid. Such was the power of the Church, of religion and politics.

I was totally absorbed in my work and finally attained my Bachelor of Arts degree. It was in my last years at university that I became a courier in the service of Her Majesty the Queen, Elizabeth. I learned of this position through a friend at the university, for there was much talk of it at the Eagle Inn where we would take sup of an evening. It was frequented by many students like myself who became drawn into the net of espionage in this way. One of the other students introduced me to a gentleman whose name was Thomas Watson. A fellow poet himself and had university friends, it was in conversation I told him how I had started to translate Lucan's First Book into English because I felt people should have the privilege to read such works. We were in agreement on this matter and as our conversation continued, we talked of my devising a new method of poetry, blank verse. He told me he was a great friend of Sir Philip Sydney and his father-in-law Sir Francis Walsingham, who was the Secretary of State. He asked me if I would like to make some extra monies and would I be interested in becoming a courier, it would be a matter of delivering a package both here and on the continent and he also offered me an invitation to visit him in London.

The next opportunity I had I visited this gentleman where he lived, it was in Shoreditch, we talked for a considerable time, into the early morning. He said he could arrange a meeting for me with Mr Secretary, next time I am in London. Mr Secretary had a network of agents around the country, the Continent and the Low Countries. When we arrived Mr Secretary was busy, but there was a young man there who was the secretary to Sir Philip and Lady Sydney, who occasionally busied himself in the Service, and said he would see me. His name was Mr Robert Poley. I knocked on the door. "Come in," he said, quite abruptly. I entered and stood before him at his desk, he signalled with his quill to sit down, still writing away. He looked up at me, a man with a mop of golden hair which fell to his shoulders, older than myself in years, and rather handsome with fine features and a neatly trimmed moustache and beard. He was dressed in black velvet doublet and breeches trimmed with gold braid and a small white ruff around his neck. He had two gold rings on his first and third fingers of his right hand… "Your name," he said.

I stumbled in reply: "Christopher Marley, Marlowe, Merlin."

"Well what is it to be then, my friend?" he said. "Is it Marlowe?", looking at me with those ice-cold blue eyes of his.

I said: "Yes". "Yes what, he interrupted." "Christopher Marlowe from Canterbury in Kent."

"Christopher Marlowe it is then," and he scibbled it down on his paper. "Why are you here?" – leaning forward and studying me.

"Mr Poley, I am here to offer my services as a courier, to be in the service of Her Majesty."

"Ah, but can we trust you?" "What are you about?"

I told him that I was studying at Benets (Corpus Christi) College in Cambridge.

"Oh, you are going to be a parson then?", sitting back in his chair. "Hmph, you don't look the type."

"Well that is what I wish to be."

"Hmph, smiled to himself, that is as maybe." A very flippant man I felt. He then said, "Would you be reliable for us? We may send for you at any time, so how may we contact you at the university?"

At first I was going to say the university, and then I thought no and said he could leave a message for me at the Eagle Inn, 'a stone's throw' from the college. His reply was, "Can the innkeeper be trusted?"

"Yes, I'm sure he can."

He then changed his whole way of conversation. "I was at Claire's you know."

"Oh," I said, "not far from where I am."

"And you?" Ah, I remember, Benets' (Corpus Christi).

"At Benets', as I said. Mine was a scholarship."

"Had to work my way through university, as I had a foolish mother. When my father died she re-married a man who squandered our money, so I had to work my way through

My Truth

college by emptying piss pots and running errands in order to carry on my studies of the Classics, he said. "Have you read Homer?"

"Yes", I replied. This started a conversation, and an interesting one at that. I found this man could be very abrupt, but felt we had a lot in common. He said to me, "Well, Christopher, we will speak again and I'm sure that we will be working together in the not-too-distant future." I looked at him, his eyes seemed cold and yet he spoke warmly. He put his hand out, across the desk, towards mine and then pulled it away. He said to me, "We'll give you a chance, a trial, but I cannot say when there is going to be work, but if there is I'll send for you. Now I must carry on with what I was doing." His head went down and he picked up his quill. "You may leave." I got up from my chair and left the room, walked down the stairs and rejoined Tom.

We visited an inn and had a meal, then left to return to college and my studies. Such a strange gentleman Mr Poley, I could not get off of my mind. It was as if he was two people, a very bitter man, a man who I wanted to know, and yet I was not sure about.

In March or April time, coming up to the Easter festivities, I decided one evening to go across to the Eagle Inn for a flagon of ale. The innkeeper put on a good fare of jugged hare and various other meals, more tasty than that at university. As I was sitting there by the fire, drinking my ale, I heard a voice, it was a voice that almost chilled me to the bone, one I recognised in an instant from my first meeting at Seething Lane.

"Christopher Marlowe," he said. 'Twas Robert Poley. I slowly turned and he was standing there, he had a dark brown cloak wrapped around him, his hair a little straggly, but still as bright as ever. He looked at me, with those ice-cold blue eyes, so cold they could chill you. It was a little like, you would call the Medusa, turn you to stone.

He then sat down. "Is there a drink for me?" I called over the pot-boy and asked him to fetch a flagon of ale for my friend. "We meet again then, Christopher. I may have some work for you, but first I want to ask you if you are willing to travel." I asked where to and he said, "Rheims". There is a seminary there for English Catholics who also wish to become priests."

So I said: "I know not much of Catholicism. I have been brought up in the Protestant ways."

"So," he said. "Well, you will have to learn then, will you not. He took out a set of rosary beads from his doublet. I know you know nothing of how to use these."

I smiled, "Nay, sir."

He in turn smiled, and then in a very cold manner, "I will have to teach you the ways of the Catholic faith, of my former religion." He spoke of this very quietly, in a stage whisper, so as not to be overheard.

Shortly after this Mr Poley said: "tomorrow evening I want you here at six of the clock and no earlier or later, then you start to learn".

I said: "Well, I may be a little late. I have my studies."

"Your studies will wait," he said. "I need you. I can't send you on a mission without the knowledge of what you are to do," he said quietly. He then took a drink of his ale. "Can you spare the time to take salt with me?"

"Yes," I said. Poley picked up his cloak and we then went downstairs.

We ate our food in silence. He asked for a finger bowl. It is as if everything had to be in its place. He asked for a napkin and said: "one must always keep clean Christopher."

"A lot of people are filthy," he said. "Unclean."

I said: "Maybe through no fault of their own."

"'Tis no excuse," he said. "You can wash in hot and cold water." He carried on with his food. He then pushed the plates aside. "Have you time to walk with me?" He drank down his wine. He wiped his fingers, moustache and beard. He placed on his cloak and we walked. He hardly spoke, just taking in the scenery, and we made our way back to the college. "Don't forget," he said, turning round to me rather abruptly, "Tomorrow evening I will be waiting for you." We parted company and I went back to my bedchamber.

I could not understand this man. He gave me the impression that he wanted to own you. He wanted your soul. He would not give you a chance to make your mind up, he made it for you. One minute he would be warm, the next he was cold. As I say, like the Medusa. He would turn you to stone with one look. I laid on my truckle bed. I could not get his face from my mind. I could see that cold look in his eyes. Maybe there is some warmth there I know not of. He was a man that one would say his countenance haunted you, and his voice. Once you made contact with him you felt that his presence never left you. And then I drifted into sleep.

Having readied myself the next day I went across to the Eagle Inn, and there he was, sitting there relaxing with a flagon of ale. He was dressed in a dark grey doublet and breeches, a white shirt with lace collar and cuffs, and a laced front. His curly hair was brushed back, his beard and moustache immaculately clipped. His eyes bore into me, a cold winter's sky blue, as he casually fingered the chain around his neck. I felt intimidated, as if I was being watched. He gestured to me to sit down and called the pot-boy over to bring me an ale. We drank, and then he said we must go upstairs. I went with him to the room, and once inside he locked the door. "We don't want anyone coming in do we?" he said. And he put the key in his pocket.

There was a fire burning in the hearth and supper laid out on the table in a corner of the room. There was himself in a chair by the fire and myself opposite. I felt unnerved, but once settled he proceeded to show me a book of cyphers – code. These were to be kept secret and I must not let the book leave my person. These I was instructed to learn as they would be my means of communication once on assignments. He said that when he next saw me he would spend some time and teach me how to use them. He said there were instructions in the book, but that if I was unsure I could ask. Previously, when visiting the headquarters of the agency at Mr Secretary's home in Seething Lane, London, I had met a very, very clever man called Mr Philippes. It was he who was the code-breaker. He could open a seal on a letter and it looked as if it had never been tampered with.

He asked me what I knew of the Catholic Church. I said I knew a little from what I heard. He said to me that I would need to know the ways of the Church and gave me notes on the Mass that I was to memorise. I was also given a wooden crucifix on a silver chain to wear when I was travelling to the continent, if needs be. This, as Robert Poley showed me, was hollow, and a small piece of parchment could be slipped inside on which I was to have written cyphered messages. Once hidden the crucifix could be exchanged for an identical one, Mr Poley himself having one such. I was also given rosary beads that he showed me how to use, threading them through his fingers and reciting a prayer on each one. 'Hail Mary, full of grace, the Lord is with me.' We said either five 'Hail Mary's' or ten 'Our Father's', whichever. It all depended if you had done any wrong. The affirmation would be said on each stone of the rosary in turn. If I remember rightly there is five beads and ten beads, for they are in sections.

He asked me if I had eaten. I said I had not. We went over and sat at the table. He was very particular about his food. He liked the table to be well set, everything in its place, and the food to be cooked properly, for he would complain if it was not. He asked me if I was to take salt on my food, which I was, and he had two bottles of wine. As we ate he asked me a few questions about myself and where I came from, but when I asked him about himself he was very distant and wary of speaking about himself. He asked me how I was for money. I replied that a student's stipend wasn't an awful lot and that was why I was looking for courier work in the service of Her Majesty, so as to make myself some extra monies. He said that my assignments would be small at first, but he suggested that if I proved satisfactory, I could find myself earning quite a lot of monies working as an agent. As a student I realised that this would present an opportunity to further supplement my small stipend. He was interested in seeing if I was prepared to involve myself with more serious duties, and he asked many questions of me for he must needs know that I could be trusted. He then said that he knew Nicholas Faunt who had gone to King's School before me, and that he also knew of my persuasion and that he would find that useful for there were a lot of Catholic priests of the same mind. He told me that he was once going to be a priest. I felt that rather strange. Being ten years older than myself he had been born during Mary's reign. She herself was a Catholic monarch, and Robert Poley's family practising Catholics.

We stayed late that evening, talking. He remarked on how handsome I was and that I could do with some better clothes. If I decided that I would like to take on more responsible assignments he suggested that I dress a little better. He went over to his saddlebag and took out of it a pouch of money.

He tipped the coins out upon the table and said: "Here, buy yourself some clothes."

I said: "I cannot possibly take this money, I have not earned it."

His reply was: "Oh, you soon will. Maybe I will give it to you as a gift ... call me Robin." He looked at me and asked how old I was, to which I replied: "22 years old." He said: Don't worry Christopher, I am older and wiser and I will take care of you and teach you all you need to know." He then returned his money pouch to his bag, and sat down again at the table. At his suggestion we finished the wine. As we did so he spoke of his travels on the Continent. He also said that he had spent time in the Marshalsea investigating Catholics who were imprisoned there, and that all agents could expect to spend some time in prison, oft times spying. He said that there were times when he took on dangerous assignments, and he asked me then if I had killed a man. I said no, it was wrong. He said that in his case it was 'kill or be killed', and that I mustn't feel bad if I had to kill another person. He asked me if I could kill him. I said no. He said: "But if I was going to kill you then you would have to kill me."

I said to him: "Have you killed men?"

"Yes, but I don't kill women and children." He then said there would come a time when I would have to kill. He said: "You may have to kill another agent, or even one of your own agents." (I count myself fortunate that that was never the case. I fought, but I never killed.) Robin said that he could kill a man, but I said: "What about him not being armed?" His reply was: "if he had to be dispatched, then he had to be dispatched whether he was armed or not. He would have to be silenced." He then said: "Leave it to me, you will see how it works." I did. "It is no trouble at all." You will think me a coward, but it made me feel sick to my stomach when I first saw it happen. I know maybe the person was wrong and that

My Truth

they could have killed us, but he never gave them a chance. He had made his decision whether they were armed or not. He was very quick, for you could be sitting there one minute and in his clutches the next. He would wait for you, as he did once with me in Dunstable.

I did something that he wasn't happy about, so later on he was waiting. He met me as I entered a dark alley and, swathed in his cloak, he raised his arm against the wall to the side of me and barred my way. He said that he had to teach me a lesson for being a 'naughty boy', but he was rather rough, for he meant business, you understand. He was the sort of man, that even though you liked him, you were never sure if he would kill you. You were on edge with him. I was taller, he was shorter in stature and thick set. I myself was a match for him. I had a fiery temper and a sharp and caustic wit, that was what he liked about me. He liked a man who stood up to him. If you didn't, and you were weak and grovelled then he had no time for you, he would kill you. He said that he hated weakness. He didn't like anyone who grovelled, 'bootlickers'. He had no time for them.

After these meetings with Robert Poley, he entrusted me with a package which I had to take to Thomas Walsingham and collect another to leave with Gilbert Gifford and a man called Christopher Blount, before entering the seminary at Rheims. My first assignment was to go to Rye in Sussex, whereupon I was to liaise with a young man, Thomas Walsingham, the cousin of Sir Francis Walsingham, Mr Secretary. My instructions were to meet him on the shore. He would be wearing a hat with a dark green feather. When I approached him I felt hesitant, not quite sure of myself, especially as he was Mr Secretary's cousin, but to my surprise, he broken the silence first. He said: "Mr Marlowe, good-day to you sir, I am Thomas Walsingham." I remember thinking, here was a young gentleman much taller than myself, medium build with fine features and a very distinctive Walsingham nose.

His doublet and breeches matched the colour of the feather in his hat and his shoes, gloves and hat were black. Around his neck he had a white collar, edged with white lace.

Sensing my uneasiness, he placed his arm upon my shoulder saying: "Well, Mr Marlowe, let us get our priorities in order first, let us visit the inn across the way, for I am sure thou must be hungry and ready to take sup with me." "I certainly am, I replied."

While at the inn (in a private room) we talked about ourselves and discovered that we had many things in common, which I must admit built up my confidence. He explained that there was a need for more couriers to travel to and from the Continent and the Low Countries, carrying letters and packages. In doing so there was always the danger of these being intercepted and falling into the wrong hands. If you decide to take up this offer, which I believe you are very capable of doing, you must take great care not to divulge your whereabouts to a soul, or you would put not only your life in jeopardy but the lives of many here in England especially our Sovereign Lady. You would be paid handsomely and I would be your cover agent along with Robert Poley. At this point I recall a feeling of excitement welling up inside of me, even though at times there would be danger, I was prepared to take that risk, for the thought of 'living on a knife edge' appealed to me, and I knew there would be no turning back. So I readily accepted Thomas' offer of more work being undercover at Rheims.

This was to be the first of many assignments away from these shores. I was a little nervous when I first took my journey to Rheims. It was at that time Thomas Walsingham was my cover agent. I had seen him briefly at Rye earlier, when he was with Robin and other men, and I was introduced to him. I wasn't sure how I would take the trip on a boat for I had never travelled by sea and I felt a little sickly – nauseous, but

My Truth

eventually, as travelling went on, I got my sea legs. On my way I went through Canterbury and saw my family, then to Dover and visited some relatives there, before travelling on to France. There was a Catholic agent called Gilbert Gifford who was mainly posted in France at the seminary in Rheims. It was a university, similar to Corpus Christi, which was for the Anglican priesthood, where British Catholics trained to become priests. I had to purport to be a Catholic sympathiser wishing to become a priest. So I had to know of the Catholic ways, and this I learned from Robin, who confessed to being a lapsed Catholic. For if you made one mistake your cover was blown. So you had to be a good actor and convince the seminary that you weren't an agent. Rheims was very beautiful, the gothic Cathedral was one of splendour filled with life-like statues of the Holy family, Saints and Apostles and the monks made very sweet wine, red being my favourite. It was while I was staying in Rheims I was thinking about another play, but I had not quite made my up my mind on its title. When I first arrived in Rheims I stayed at some lodgings and it was there I met Thomas Walsingham my cover agent. There wasn't a relationship with us at that time, we were just working together as agent and cover agent. I was concentrating on Gilbert Gifford, for I had to hand over letters to him from Sir Francis Walsingham.

When I moved into the seminary I shared a room with a young priest named François, much devoted to his faith. On observing him for sometime, I discovered that he would be a very fine candidate, so it would not be long before I could have him 'eating out of my hand'. In our many conversations he told me much about himself and revealed that there were many who hated that heretic bitch who sits on the English throne. I remember him saying that he came from the Loire Valley where his father owned a small vineyard. This priest become a close ally and confidant in the time I was in exile and working for Sweet Robin, who took great pains to explain to me the need to know the Holy Sacraments and how to use the rosary beads as regards to uttering the amount of Our Father's and Hail Mary's. He said: "You would be instructed on how many of these to say, once you have been to confession." The priest gave me a small scourge telling me that if unclean thoughts entered one's mind you were to flog yourself. As a priest you must remain celibate, a rule I found extremely difficult to uphold at times, as I would have had no flesh left if I scourged myself for the thoughts in my mind. Fortunately for me though, the lectures kept me busy, but there were those who were caught and killed. Now, I had one advantage because I was a student of Divinity at Corpus Christi, so I knew of the Scriptures and I read the Classics. A confession I wasn't too happy with, although at that time in my life there wasn't a lot to confess. (A wry chuckle) I was also told by Robin that you had to be celibate to become a priest, something François had explained to me and then he laughed: "Hmph, he said there would be many pretty young priests there to entertain me. Or choirboys, whichever (Laughing at himself), but I had to keep my mind on what I was doing."

Speaking French was no problem, as I had two friends back in Canterbury who were French, and you can pick up the language as you go along. There were lots of plots at this time to assassinate Queen Elizabeth and put Mary of Scots on the throne of England. What I had to do was listen to what had been said in the seminary with the other students. I had to listen in on conversations, and listen in taverns. You have a conversation, but your ear is elsewhere, then you listen to what has been said and you report it back. Anything that was detrimental I would give it to Thomas to be passed over. There were ways, and you had to be careful. We would exchange crucifixes. We would have secret pockets in our doublet; and later on I had a mirror in my sleeve so I could see who was behind me. You had to be very careful. As a courier it wasn't

My Truth

so dangerous. When I was at the seminary they had had a man called Richard Baines infiltrating there. He was another agent, but he made a mess of things. He tried to poison the wells at the seminary, but then got caught. He was a fool, and he turned informer on me later on. He never listened to what he was briefed. He thought he could do one better than others, and not just with myself, but, not thinking, he would go and blow the cover.

While there I attended lectures, and I had to go to confession, and there were the Hail Mary's, and the prayers, and the masses, but there were secret meetings as well where they would swear allegiance to Mary and to the Pope, and 'death to the bastard, Queen Elizabeth', which was wrong. Myself I did not think it was right to stop a person having their beliefs and their faith if it was what they were happy with, and they were practising their belief in the privy of their home and doing no harm to anyone else. That is all good and well, but if they are plotting against the country then it is wrong. The more I learned about the plots and the counter plots the more I saw of this. As I got older and stood back and looked at religion, and used my psychic side, I saw the fanaticism on both sides. Sir Francis Walsingham was a fanatic for destroying Mary, and the Catholic Church was fanatical in destroying Elizabeth. So really neither of them was any better than the other. I feel that in some ways although Sir Francis was trying to protect his queen, and I understand that and respect his loyalty, that he could have dealt with it a little fairer. For he spared no mercy for any priests if they were captured. Some of them, methinks myself, were not plotting against the Queen, they were just visiting Catholic houses and being what they were, which was priests, but once they were in Topcliffe's hands – oh! (He shudders) – their own mothers wouldn't know them.

At that time I did not realise how deep into the net I was falling. I spent many absences on the Queen's business carrying letters and packages around the country and on the continent, including Rheims, Flushing and The Hague.

One evening, when I was leaving my residence at the seminary to 'take some air', in the shadows I spied a figure but to my joy it was Thomas Walsingham. He quickly grabbed my arm and ushered me down the street. "Keep walking" he said, for we need to be out of ear-shot from those who may be spying on thee. He asked if I had anything to report. "Nothing", I replied, except there was bitterness against our Queen, though nothing as yet could you describe as being a plot, but I have managed to gain the trust of a priest named François. Thomas told me I must ask those at the seminary for leave, as I was needed to take an urgent letter back to England. He would meet me on the morrow, so that I could leave in good time on the early tide.

On my return to England I was to take the letter to Seething Lane, the headquarters of Mr Secretary, Sir Francis Walsingham. Upon my arrival I was ushered into his study. This was the second occasion I had a private meeting with him, he was a man who 'never suffered fools gladly'. It was true how the Queen described him as her 'Moor', for he had a swarthy complexion. On his head was a skullcap and he was wearing a long fur-trimmed burgundy robe over his doublet. He said: "Pray be seated Mr Marlowe". I believe you have a letter for me do you not. Hand it here to me please. After handing the letter to him he rang a brass bell on his desk. I remember another door to the study opening and in stepped a rather short, thin-faced fair-haired man, dressed all in grey. Sir Francis handed him the letter I had brought and addressed him by the name of Thomas Phelippes. The young man took from his pocket a pair of glass-eyes and began to carefully peruse each line before scurrying back to his room. After which Sir Francis then asked me if I had heard of cyphers. I replied: "Yes, Mr Poley had instructed me on their use." At that moment Sir Francis produced a small book from a box lying on his desk. He explained: "to a layman this book means nothing, but to an agent it is considered a life-line". He further said: "My cousin Thomas had been praising thee on your first assignment. I remember our first conversation Mr Marlowe, you mentioned you was a poet and playmaker." This would be most useful, particularly the poetry, for it could contain hidden messages within the lines of verse. Sir Francis thought that this form of cypher would be quite unique.

At this meeting I was instructed to return to Rheims with a reply placed inside a hollow wooden crucifix and issued with a ring that was also hollow and handy for concealing a poison or sleeping draught. Sir Francis asked me to remain close to his cousin Thomas at all times, for he could be in danger.

This was the start of many assignments I was involved in on the Continent both with Thomas Walsingham and Robert Poley and as it turned out this assignment led to the uncovering of a major plot to kill the queen and place Mary of Scots on the throne.

Other times, as a courier in England, I was given packages that I had to deliver to certain parts of the country, stay at an inn and then wait for a reply. There were times when I did not have replies, and not always was there an inn to sleep in, so I would sleep in a barn. I was loaned a horse if needs be. This bought me little monies so I could pay for extra food, books, paper, or whatever I needed. I found this intriguing and when Mr Poley came back from his travels I would visit him at the Eagle Inn, where he would stay. We spent many hours where he would teach me his cyphers and I decided that I, if given the privilege, could send code in my poems, in a small rhyme. I worked very hard at understanding the various codes, letters and such. You could antamogorise, turn words around the other way, for in the School of Night we used to say 'dog' instead of God. I found my work very intriguing.

Upon my return to university I was told that due to my absences I was not going to be awarded my Master's degree, and if I wished to continue I would have to remain a further year before they would reconsider me for it. This infuriated me, for I tried to explain my reasons, but was told they were not acceptable. So therefore I visited Mr Secretary, Sir Francis Walsingham, at his residence, Barn Elms, to ask him to intervene and make it possible for the university authorities to reconsider. He did this for me and I was granted my Master's degree in 1587. I then told the authorities I had no desire to be ordained, for within my heart I knew I would be going against my own principles and that I would be a hypocrite if I did so. Reluctantly my decision was accepted, for Mr Secretary intervened, and my obligation to be ordained was waived. Of course my parents were disappointed, my mother mainly. She felt that I had let her down and wasted her love and energy, but most of all I had let God down. I explained to her that I would not have been happy living the life of a clergyman and that my path was that of a poet and playmaker. My university education was now to be channelled through my writing.

Chapter 3

The Playmaker

The day I finally left university, it was like being released from a cage, for like an animal I felt ensnared. At last I was free, a free spirit allowed to express myself in my poetry and writing, thus bringing colour into people's lives that were otherwise full of nothing but poverty and misery. For by this time I had already taken London by storm with my mighty 'Tamburlaine', which I started to write in the mid-1580s. It was accepted and first performed at the 'Curtain' theatre. In later years it was performed at the 'Rose' theatre on Bankside. It was a great success and Edward Alleyn, the principal actor, persuaded me to write a follow up which I called 'Tamburlaine the Great'. That too was a true success, and it took London by storm.

One of my first attempts at playmaking was with another university student, Thomas Nashe, from Lowestoft. The play was called 'Dido, Queen of Carthage'. I wrote another play about a conqueror whose name was Skanderberg, but I lost interest in it for it would not come together as I wished, but I hoped to finish it in later years. There was a further play, 'The Jew of Malta', which I also started to write at university and later completed with the help of Thomas.

It was 1587 when I left university. Between times I had made an acquaintance with Thomas Watson who lived in Norton Folgate, not far from Hogg Lane, near Spitalfields. He was a fellow poet and a good friend of Sir Francis Walsingham and his son-in-law Sir Philip Sydney, married to his daughter Frances, who later became patron to Thomas Watson. Tom Watson offered me a room in his house, which I gladly accepted. It was a small room at the back of his house, just below the garret. It had a single truckle bed, but very comfortable with linen sheets and claret-coloured coverlet. In front of the window was a table which had on it an iron candlestick, and beside the table was a chair. Above the window was a single curtain on a rod, the same colour as the coverlet. The fireplace had a wooden mantle and on it was another iron candlestick. Next to the fireplace was a table with a jug a pitcher and beside the bed was a chamber pot and at the bottom of the bed was a trunk for my clothes. It was a large house and he let the rooms, although at that time I was his only lodger. I furnished it modestly with cushions, which I loved, these were a gift from mother and other little luxuries to make me feel comfortable. I always had a good fire in the hearth on winter evenings. I couldn't thank Tom enough for his kindness.

Tom introduced me to Thomas Kydd and those of the theatre and it was through him that my first play, 'Tamburlaine' was presented. Tom was married in the latter part of our friendship, although I didn't see her very much, as she was always with her sister-in-law Ann Poley. She was very pretty and rather timid, slight in figure with a rounded face and her cheeks blushed a rosy pink. Her eyes, large and brown and framed with a mop of amber-coloured hair. Tom was a good friend, who accepted me as a fellow poet and playmaker. I was able to discuss my writings and plays with him for he would be my critic, but his criticism was of a constructive nature and therefore spurred me on to write more. He told

My Truth

me of his stay in France when Sir Francis Walsingham was the English ambassador, and of the St Bartholomew's Day Massacre, which inspired me to write 'The Massacre at Paris'. I spent much of my time in my room writing, that's if I wasn't delivering packages for Sir Francis, I would also visit my friends, and methinks Robert Poley was in the Tower at this time for what was to be a two year stay. I visited him, collecting letters to be delivered to Sir Francis, for Robert was informing on political prisoners.

I would spend my time researching histories, and I owned a copy of 'The Holinshed Chronicles' to assist me in my research. Thomas Walsingham was not my patron then but I had support from my wages as a courier, and revenue from my play, when I was paid. I spent most of my time working in my lodgings, and would oft times share a meal with Tom and his wife. Other times I would eat with friends, or go to an inn, the 'Cross Keys', not far from Tom's lodgings. At this time I was continuing my other task, which was translating Lucan's First Book and Ovid's Elergies into English. I began these works in the latter part of my university years and they took me about a year and a half to complete. I have always been of the opinion that the common man should be able to read for himself, for it was unfair that a man could not read well enough on his own and especially the classics such as Ovid that was traditionally written in Latin. I felt that everyone should be able to read it and have equal opportunities. I also believed women should also be educated. For myself I felt that if a woman is worthy of it why should she not learn, for she too has a brain, so why not give her the same opportunity as a man. I believed she should use it, and not just be there for procreation, this is something I often argued with my male friends, for 'there is no sin but ignorance'. When giving tuition to middle-class families' children I found that in some cases they were very bright, and some were girls too. Middle-class families could afford the tuition, but for others a fee would have to been paid at school and then perhaps scholarships awarded to go to university, but only for the boys. All ladies of the house and daughters of the gentry were educated, so that they became good housekeepers. The church provided schools for children; and the bishops provided the scholarships, but I wanted to give education to poor children and it was a pity that girls did not have the same opportunity. In the theatre there were boys who could read and write, but who had not received a university education. I would give my time in the afternoons to teach them how to read blank verse and help with their acting skills.

It was while I was at the theatre one day, I first met William Shakespeare in rehearsal at the 'Curtain' in London, working behind the scenes and taking small acting parts with the theatre group. We were both 25 years old, and unlike myself who had been university educated, he was not a well-educated man, but his flair for writing had drawn him to the theatre. Unbeknown to him I had been in the gallery during rehearsals for a play and watched him stumble over several of his lines. He was finding it difficult to read the script with the smooth flow demanded by the rather arrogant leading actor, Edward Alleyn. He was much angered at finding himself the butt of Alleyn's scathing humour, and threw down his script and strode from the stage. I found myself intrigued by this tempestuous young man and called after him, having first rebuked Alleyn for his haughty outburst. An overly confident actor he would take it upon himself to change lines in plays as he saw fit, but that was the right of the censors, not actors, and I informed him in no uncertain terms that other than the censors, changes in my plays were my decision and mine alone. "Without the playmaker you do not have the play." After apologising for Alleyn's overbearing manner I introduced myself to William Shakespeare as the playmaker, Christopher Marlowe, and was greeted by the surprised expression on the now becalmed young actor's face. It appeared he was in

My Truth

awe of me as a leading poet and playmaker of the time, and feeling an instant affinity with him, invited him to join me for victuals at the Cross Keys inn. As we became engrossed in conversation I realised that before me sat an intelligent man with a sharp mind, wit and creative intelligence. He told me as a youth he had wanted to continue his studies and maybe enter university, but had not been encouraged to do so by his father, who insisted he join him in the family business. He married at 18 years of age to a lady who was with child, for what was to the imaginative Shakespeare, a life of numbing mundaneness. The opportunity to seek his fortune as an actor, and his subsequent meeting with me put him on a path of learning and creative self-expression as a fellow playmaker. Observing his sharp wit and humour, and astute observation of human nature and its foibles, coupled with a flair for writing, I recognised in him the potential for greatness as a writer of comedies. It was I who was to tutor him in all that I knew for he was a willing, patient and industrious pupil; and I an able teacher.

Unable to afford lodgings he was sleeping rough in the tiring rooms of the theatre as some actors, short of funds, were apt to do. Realising that there was a deep bond of friendship between us at the time, I offered for Will to share my lodgings. A truckle bed came into use in my chamber and we lived and worked as true friends.

Prior to that Thomas Kydd had lodged with me who was a talented playmaker. He was a quiet man who sought little company, and we came together through our love of writing. It was later to develop into a short-lived physical relationship, but I fear my impetuosity when writing, and volatility, led to our eventual parting a year later. I was a man who felt inspired to write at night beyond the midnight hour, and I would invariably wake Thomas to enthuse about my writing and to read aloud to him when he would have preferred to sleep. Then come morning I would be weary and sleep late into the day, oft times waking bad-tempered and moody. Ultimately Thomas found himself lacking the tolerance and understanding that eventually Will brought, with his friendship, to marry my Piscean nature. 'Sweet Will' I was to call him. We were twin souls, born in the same year and destined to meet.

If I had an argument I would not let it go, I would bring it all back. 'Tis wrong, I know that. Will would tell me it was wrong to bear a grudge unless it was something damaging to me. Will believed in dealing with a situation and clearing it, for he did not bear grudges, he said life was short enough.

Will was very studious once he got involved with my tutoring. I was prepared to give time to him and he was punctual and eager to learn. He would write lines for plays, give me ideas and points of view to help me. I was never destructive in my criticism. I would ask why he had come up with an idea and how it would work on stage. In each play we would create a plot, and once it was written we would act it out because of time restrictions. The crowd loved duels and action. I believed in keeping my audiences attention and in 'Tamburlaine' a chariot was ridden across the stage. "In my plays you never fell asleep." Will was later to help me tutor the young boys of the theatre, as I indeed tutored him.

I was angry with fathers who wanted their children to go into the family trade, or worse to beg and steal. Mothers wanted their children to be educated, but they were 'under the thumb' of their husbands. A lot of cut-purses were children, and parents would disfigure and maim their own children for begging. I was appalled. If you were willing to put yourself out, there was work to be found. For me it was a great sadness to see ability wasted in such a way. There were rent boys and girls selling their bodies to live. I would never lay with a boy under 14 years old, for I did not think it proper. Others did, but not I, but apart from my personal feelings, learning was most important. I could not live without my books, even in exile. Tom Watson agreed with me that education was important. Women were educated in my time, but could not take up positions. They could be nannies or governesses, but they were not allowed to teach. Another thing I did not agree with, was for a tutor to beat the children. A child could not learn by fear, for he was more likely to be resentful. I was fortunate myself to have had good tutors, although I had seen violence in my youth, I didn't agree with it. I believed in being constructive, not destructive. I would look for a child's potential, but I could not make them a scholar if it was not there. I noticed that some children had difficulty in their learning, but I always did my best to guide them, for I had a lot of patience with children and those who wanted to learn, despite their background.

Philip Henslowe, who owned the 'Rose' theatre and other places, had his 'fingers in many pies', but was illiterate. He was not a man of learning, for I could see this, so he put on an act, but he could not fool me. So long as money was coming in he wasn't bothered. My main concern was the welfare of the boys for they acted in the plays and were seen by men who would buy them for the evening, or the night, from Henslowe. He took the payment for himself and in return the boys were given food and were allowed to sleep in the theatre. If they refused they were beaten up by several men who were often sadistic, rough and cruel, so I tried to help them, by teaching them to defend themselves.

Philip Henslowe owned brothels in the stews and in one of his brothels he kept boys dressed in gowns to please the gentlemen who came to the theatre, and he would also have his best whores in the theatre on the evening. The theatre would get very, very tightly packed. There were the groundlings who stood up during the performance, and you could pay extra in the stalls if you wanted to have a cushion to sit down. They used to sell bags of hazelnuts. I myself would sit on the stage, for as the playmaker it was my privilege. I would always

Brenda Harwood

make sure I made my attendance at the first performance as Ned Alleyn would oft times change the lines, which I did not approve, as it was not his place to do so without having my permission. Once, I stopped a performance, although Philip was not too pleased, but as far as I was concerned it was the last time Ned Alleyn was going to do this to me. If he wanted to try his hand at playmaking that was up to him, but I was the playmaker and you do not alter my words. Also the Sonnets, it incenses me to hear the Sonnets have been replaced with 'she' instead of 'he'. The Sonnets were not written for women! How dare they do such a thing? Those were words of love. I do not wish them to have women mentioned. Not that I have anything against women, but they were not words of love intended for a woman. Who dared to alter it? Did Will Shakespeare? Methinks he wouldn't, for he used to send them to the Earl of Southampton. For you see I wrote them, well not all of them, for Will to send to him, for he was Will's paramour. What I wish is that they be changed back, for what I have written, I do not wish it to be changed in any way. When I wrote 'Corinna' I was thinking of a man, so I had to put a woman in his place, but I was then at Corpus Christi. In 'Hero and Leander', Thomas Walsingham was in my mind. If you read my work you will always see that whenever I speak of a man, I take great pains to write about him in detail. I remember writing the Sonnets on the Continent. If you read the Sonnets, I mention about my leaving the country when I had to take my leave. Yes, I am aware that we are going away from what we had been talking about, but it has been here within my heart for a long time, the pain has been too hard for me to bear, so I have had to speak of it.

It was about this time that I was translating works as well. In the mid-1580s I wrote 'Tamburlaine', 'Tamburlaine the Great', and 'The Massacre at Paris'. 'The Massacre at Paris' was about the St Bartholemew's Day Massacre, I also wrote 'The Jew of Malta' which was about a greedy Jew, and then there was 'Edward II', 'Dr Faustus', and in between that 'Dido of Carthage'. Actually I wrote 'Dr Faustus' in 1592, but I was also working on other plays between times. What I used to do is write parts of plays and then put them away, going back to them later on, or Will and I would work together. I was also translating 'Lucan's First book' and 'Ovid's 'Elegies' – "Amores".

London at midnight was really quiet, so I would oft times wait until the midnight hour, before I could write. I preferred a garret room as the stench rises from the streets, the garret room being furthest away. In the garret I was away from other tenants and people would have ceased their fighting. Yes, there were times I would return to my chamber having drank too much and was unable to write and would fall asleep on my bed in the clothes I stood up in. However, if I had a lover with me that would be different, all together another matter, it would give me good reason to stay awake.

So long as I had paper, pens and ink I was happy... and I had my best clothes. My favourite colours were green, brown, purple and burgundy a little. One doublet which I very much liked, was dark olive green and it was inset with deep purple panels. There were breeches, stockings and a hat to match. Woollen stockings for winter, but when I was going anywhere important my stockings were made of silk. Thomas would give me clothes, the ones he didn't want, but he had some made for me. A few of my shirts were silk given to me by Thomas and Sir Walter, but others were made of linen. To deodorise you would rub a mixture of oranges and lavender against your skin. We did wash, and I more often than some preferred to wash, as I had been brought up that way. I would take a bathe more often than Her Majesty, was very fond of musk and would use perfumes and creams scented with musk or lavender, the very strong musk rose of which I was particularly fond. Having bathed, I would rub oils into my body, or if I was fortunate somebody else would. It proves, my friend, that I was human.

I loved to walk alone in the park, oft times deep in thought, for it was in those times I would be inspired with many ideas on what to write next in my works. On my return I would sit in my room at the lodgings and meditate. There were times when nothing would come into my mind, only anger and frustration. Yes, I was angry and frustrated, in ill-humour, and would often be in my cups too much and sometimes go about looking for trouble.

Chapter 4
The Babington Plot

It was in the mid-1580s when I was absent from university, on Her Majesty's business. Methinks it was the end of March when I had a visit from a courier with a letter from Robert telling me that he wanted to meet with me and would I make myself available. It was to be at our usual meeting place in Cambridge and I was to be briefed on evidence that the Catholics in France were plotting. Robert himself had made a friend of a young man called Sir Anthony Babington who had a large estate near Matlock in Derbyshire. Robert asked if I would care to visit Sir Anthony with him. I thought about it, then said that I would go. And so it was then we visited this young man at his home.

On arrival at his home, Babington Hall, we were directed to a set of rooms on the second floor where he had a secret room. I was introduced to him as another Catholic sympathiser wishing to assist in the assassination of Queen Elizabeth, and that I was willing to take messages and carry letters. I found this man very taken with Robert. They were very close and Sir Anthony would take his hand and make a fuss of him. He was a pretty young man a little older than myself, soft features, slim and delicate. He was gentle and friendly, a generous man who if you said you liked something he would give it to you, or he would get it for you. I said that I needed paper for I loved to write poetry, and he gave me paper and pens. He made you feel welcome. He was such a kind person. He was not to me the sort of man who would want to kill a queen. I felt he was being manipulated by others, particularly a man called Father Ballard. Sir Anthony was a devout Catholic in a lot of ways, but he had his weaknesses.

He said that he was going to France to make contacts, but that he needed a passport and papers to leave the country. Robert said that he would deal with this for him and that he would take him to see Mr Secretary. Robert was to say that Sir Anthony was helping to 'sniff out' the Catholics, and Anthony Babington went along with this. But really Anthony was being trapped. Robert had been sent to encourage him to reveal more about those who were plotting against Elizabeth, saying that he was on Anthony's side. But then taking Anthony Babington to meet Sir Francis Walsingham saying that Anthony was a double agent wanting to help the cause by being a man of Catholic connections that could give information. Robert had told Sir Anthony to pretend that he would betray his fellow conspirators once details of the plot were confirmed. So besotted was he with Robert that he failed to see the dangers before him. You see Robert had Anthony where he wanted him. I could see the innocence in the man, but Robert told me I was not a parson and not to act like one. Maybe I was seeing the good side of the man and not the other side.

I will tell you now of Anthony Babington who was working, methinks with six other conspirators along with Father Ballard. It was a plot to assassinate the Queen and put Mary Queen of Scots on the throne of England. It was a time when the Protestants were ruling, for Elizabeth I was a Protestant queen, and there was unrest amongst the Catholics, especially in the North of England. Babington's home, his country seat of Babington Hall, was in Derbyshire, and Robert Poley and I were both posted on intelligence looking for information as to the movements of Anthony and his written communications to Mary. All letters were intercepted, and the letters that were intercepted from Mary I was asked to add words to in forged handwriting, because Sir Francis Walsingham, head of the spy network, wanted to make the conspiracy appear to be deeper, for he was obsessed with being rid of Mary and Catholics. He would not rest until she was dead. And on one letter from Mary about Elizabeth I was asked to draw a gibbet. Mary saw Elizabeth as a bastard, not the rightful queen, but it was others who instigated the plot against Elizabeth with Anthony Babington's support. But he was a very foolish man, he was not cunning enough, or clever enough. He blabbed about it to too many people and was too trusting, especially of his friend Robert Poley, who was getting passports and papers to enable Anthony to travel to France to meet with other Catholic supporters. Robert and myself went with him to see Sir Francis to apply for a passport and this would have cost £300. Robert had contacts in the forgery business, so people would have to be paid, and Robert himself would have taken a large percentage. In asking for the passport to visit Catholic sympathisers abroad Anthony was walking into danger.

Prior to that a meeting I had been held with the six conspirators, Father Ballard, and we all went for a meal, myself and Robert. There was much table talk, and discussion on what was going to be done. Robert and I were pretending to be sympathisers, and then we passed on information.

Yet the original idea of the plot came from Sir Francis Walsingham and it was he who engineered it. He had started the network and in his study he had a map of Europe with markers where all his agents were. He was a Puritan and had a strong hatred of Catholics. He was so intent on being rid of the Queen of Scots and the Catholicism she represented that he instigated the plot and he had no concern as to how unpleasant it became for those involved through his manipulations. Nor did he care how many lives were forfeited. Just as Anthony Babington was being used, so were the other conspirators as they were manipulated by Walsingham and his spies. There was talk of support from Mendoza, the Spanish ambassador, in France. But these men were passionate Catholics connected with the seminaries in France. I had done cover work over there with another spy, Gilbert Gifford, and I knew of the strength of feeling for the Catholic religion as the true faith. Of course after his part in all this he was safely shipped off to France, back to the seminaries spying again.

Sir Francis told Robert that he, through the spy network, had to encourage these men, in turn through Anthony Babington, to form a conspiracy. So Robert was instrumental in doing so, and I had to do the same. There were murmurings and undercurrents, but these men could not have thought to succeed in their plotting without the backing of Anthony Babington's money, for they themselves did not have the means.

Sir Francis needed as much evidence as he could to hold against Mary, so he thought of a counter-plot; thus digging her deeper which he did through his agents. He knew that Anthony Babington was infatuated with Mary, ever since her was a page in her household, and a secret Catholic. Babington was impressionable and Sir Francis used this knowledge for his own ends. He knew that if he was encouraged, the plot would thicken and also flush out all the Catholic sympathisers and priests who were plotting to place Mary on the throne of England.

It started off with Gilbert Gifford, who was of course a spy in the pay of Sir Francis, befriending Mary, telling her that she could send letters to her friends and on the continent. In writing to such people as Father Ballard they were encouraged to England and they came just as traveling priests, holding Mass in secret and under false identity. It was then up to

Walsingham's spies, such as Robert and myself, to encourage Anthony Babington to invite these priests to join him in his plot not only to assassinate the Queen but her whole government. Sharing the same aspirations they believed that they could carry through their plot successfully. They wished to see Mary free, and as queen, and having the right contacts it was possible to carry this out.

Sir Francis had Phelippes, and other men within his service, including Thomas, forge letters from the Spanish ambassador and others as words of encouragement in support of Mary. The conspirators would be thinking that these were letters coming from great men. But they were not. And there was no way of checking for letters took a long time to come from various places. He also had Mary's letters intercepted and paragraphs added to them. Indeed Mary herself never mentioned the plot to kill Queen Elizabeth, her cousin, for Mary would have wanted no part in such. The only plot that Mary knew of was to secure her release and her ultimate escape to France. So one could say that Sir Francis Walsingham not only fooled us, but he also fooled the Queen of England. He controlled and Elizabeth believed him.

I know more about the plot than people think. In forging parts of Mary's letters it was Sir Francis's way of keeping me under control. It was the way with all of his spies and those with whom he worked. It was his way of manipulating them for his own ends. He was such a powerful man that, caught in his web, one had to go along with him or be destroyed. Sir Francis had a very suspicious mind that did not allow him to trust anyone. If he didn't have something on someone he would find it or create it because he had to feel that he had ultimate control. There was an element of fear too, for he never forgot the St Batholomew's Massacre. Indeed Thomas was only safe because Sir Francis had no sons of his own and he therefore took Thomas to school like himself. He had hopes of Thomas becoming the next Secretary of State. However, that position had already been promised to Robert Cecil. Before his death he destroyed some of his files for they would have incriminated him through his involvement and manipulation of situations. He gave many of them to Thomas for safekeeping and they died with him. My instructions were to lure unsuspecting men at Court into bed. When interviewed by Sir Francis he found me stimulating, interesting, intellectual – the man that he was looking for. A good speaker, a charmer, a man befitted for the purpose he had earmarked for me. I was first introduced to the Service through my work as a courier, then given more important work before being handed over to Robert Poley for the Babington Plot. I had of course worked with Robert before in Rheims, where I also met Thomas Walsingham, as a member of the spy network. Sir Francis favoured me whenever I went on assignment and I was discreetly followed by a cover agent. In my case Robert or Thomas. I encouraged Will into it too, as a spy. At first he did not realise that I was an agent, for I used him to pass on information, which he was willing to do to help a friend. He had a great admiration for me and would do anything to please me.

Sir Francis Walsingham was a very cunning man. He would encourage you into his company, making you feel comfortable, for he loved poetry and music, and was fond of the Arts and Classics. He was like a spider, inviting you into his web. As a university man I was just what he wanted, as I mentioned before. In fact, he asked Robert's opinion of me from my interviews. He also asked Thomas if I was to be trusted and was told that I was a man of integrity. However, the one thing that I did do, that would not have been deemed appropriate, was to warn Anthony Babington. But I was doing that for Robert, and because I felt that Anthony was a foolish man who was being used, not just by one side, but by both, a man being manipulated, and realised that the only way for him to survive was to leave the country. Because he chose not to escape until it was too late, he was hunted down like a fox. In his naïvity he believed that the Queen would keep him under house arrest, and she may have softened. But Sir Francis was going to make sure that he was made an example of. The Queen herself only wanted Sir Anthony to be executed, to be beheaded as a nobleman. But it was to be no mercy for him, only torture and eventually death.

Sir Francis interrogated Robert, myself and Thomas regarding the matter even though he knew we had acted for him, but an interrogation by Sir Francis was not pleasant for he had to make sure. He had our rooms searched to see if there was anything incriminating to be found, such as heretical pamphlets. If that was the case we had to be able to explain the reason why they were in our possession. Even the rosary had a little disc that could be opened for cyphers to be inserted into. He would destroy you, for he always said: "You don't get away from me. I am behind you wherever you are. You don't go for a piss, I'll be there." He would have an agent follow an agent; plots within plots, he said there were those who would or could be persuaded to betray their master.

I had taken it upon myself to get back Robert's and Anthony's intimate letters to save Robert from himself, for I am sure he would certainly have been implicated as a traitor. Of course in obtaining them I should not have read them, but alas I did. The letter was still in my possession at my death. I did keep one, although the others would have been destroyed by Robert.

I read in one letter that poor fool Sir Anthony believed that Sir Walter Raleigh would protect him by speaking to the Queen, if all else failed. I think not, for he was only interested in his lands and moveables and made full sure that he poured only poisoned words in the Queen's ear. Sir Walter was the Queen's favourite and she hung on his every word. Babington was not the strongest of them all, it was Father Ballard and the other Catholic conspirators. You see Mary was nothing like Queen

Elizabeth, she had been sheltered at the French Court, not like Bess who lived in fear of her life. Although Mary Stuart was strong-minded like her cousin, that I could see, she was ageing but still kept her beauty. She captured the hearts of men, and I am remorseful for being made to add wicked words to her letters thus implicating her deeper in the plot. I carried this on my conscience, for I contributed to her death too. Robert Poley was looking out for letters to and from her, having them intercepted, he had his part to play as did I, but it was not upon his instruction that they be altered, rather that of Sir Francis and Thomas Walsingham. Robert was seeking information from Anthony thus passing it through Thomas to Sir Francis. You see, Sir Anthony Babington was trying to play it two ways. If the plot failed he would throw himself at the queen's mercy, for Sir Francis had reassured him that the queen would show mercy on him when he was arrested if he gave the names of the other conspirators. But this was not the truth, for Francis was out for blood and he was not bothered whose innocent blood he spilt.

To many of her followers Mary gave a brooch. The design was of a swan with a crown around its neck and a chain attached. She embroidered the design on many of her possessions for she was the captured swan, Sir Anthony often spoke about her in this way. It was through Sir Anthony that I got to know Mary and that was how I also came to feel compassionate for her. Anthony Babington had one such brooch which he gave to me to give to Robert, thinking him to be true in his support of the Catholic cause, but when I offered it to Robert he would not take it. Robert and I had met at The Grapes, an inn in Southgate, London, before Anthony Babington was to be arrested. When Anthony learnt that the plot had been discovered and that arrests to be made, he had escaped to friends in St John's Wood, London. He hid out there for three or four days or more before his arrest when he was found in hiding. He was planning to escape, but his whereabouts were discovered.

He was the last of the conspirators to be captured. As a titled man he should have been beheaded, but Sir Francis wanted to make an example of him, so he was executed like a common traitor in mid-September along with his conspirators who were taken out for their execution. They were hung, drawn and quartered, dragged through the streets and tortured. Topcliffe spared no mercy. They would tie you up on a post by your wrists and your feet with manacles. Occasionally they would put a stool under your feet, unless they let you hang, and there was fire run up and down your body with torches. They would stick knives in you, not enough to kill you, and down your genitals, and there was the rack, everyone feared the rack. They would break your knuckles, break your knees with a hammer, pull out your fingernails, and put a band around your head and tighten it. There are various means of torture – Babington and the other conspirators were hung by the neck for so long and then cut down, and their genitals cut off with a rusty blade while they were still alive, thrown into the fire and then they would have their bowels removed. Topcliffe once did this and mind you I was not there, he skipped with them. Then they would cut your body into four quarters, cut off your legs and your arms and then your head. The four quarters would be hung up in various places, north, south, east and west, their heads stuck on a spike for all to see. Not a very pleasant spectacle... You are unrecognisable by then. It does make you think and waken you to the thought of what you may be getting into.

In some ways I felt sorry for Anthony Babington for he was a foolish man plotting to kill our sovereign Queen and to overthrow her government. He said that it was not his idea to kill her, but Father Ballard's, and that he got carried away with it all. I told him to leave the country. He could have gone as a stowaway or got away whichever way he chose, and had he gone earlier he would not have been detected, as they would not have been looking for him. But alas he remained, because he trusted people. He thought by offering to give up of the conspirators, he would have saved himself, but you see he was a very foolish man. He was too impressionable and impetuous. The conspirators used him because he was wealthy and could finance everything. Once the plot was underway he could pay for armies and whatever was needed. The other men, Father Ballard and Titchbourne, were the ones who were actually using him for their own ends. He was the man with the fat purse and he was easily flattered. And Robert Poley too was good at that. Sweet Robin charmed his way into his life and his bed and took him for a fool.

But I had got to know Anthony for Robert would go off and leave me there with him sometimes. He was gregarious, a man who loved people around him and he was generous. But, as Robert put it, he had to be ensnared, caught in the web. But I found him interesting company, charming, a delightful man in a very gentle way. If you hurt yourself he was very attentive and thoughtful. But he was so believing that Father Ballard and John Savage were going to assassinate the Queen, that Mary was going to become the queen and that everything was going to be a bed of roses. He was seeing everything as if it was all going to be easy. I told him that the Queen Elizabeth is well-loved and he was a fool to think England would not suffer another ruler like Bloody Mary. But he insisted that this Mary would be tolerant of all religions.

I looked at him and said: "are you so naïve to think that England would remain in peace, the protestants have long memories and will not forget what a Catholic ruler put them through in years past".

He would not change his mind on that subject, he then went to speak of Sweet Robin and how he would support him all the way in his cause. I then thought to myself. Poor Sir Anthony,

Sweet Robin has you for a fool. He has truly ensnared him and from what I can see, Anthony Babington has dug a hole which he will never get out of and as good as signed his own death warrant.

Sir Anthony was studying law at the Inner Temple. We used to meet at the Cross Keys and various other inns, in the upper rooms with all the other conspirators, but I only took despatches here and there. I did not realise how deep the relationship was between Robin and Sir Anthony, until one evening I returned with a letter for Robin and the door to their chamber had not been locked. I burst in on them, only to find each in an amorous embrace. I retreated hastily and shut the door behind me. I had suspected there was a closeness between them but had not thought it had gone so far. I sat in the other room then Robin came out to me from the bedchamber. Putting his hands gently upon my shoulder and began to whisper in my ear. Pillow-talk my friend. I have him where I want him, sorry if I embarrassed you, but I don't love him, it is part of the game. He said: "What do you have for me?" I took the packet from my doublet and slipped into his hand. He then opened the letter, read its contents and after threw it onto the fire. From that day onward Robin never hid his charade with Anthony from me.

I knew Robin had a mistress, her name was Joan Yeoman and a married woman to boot. He also had a wife, her name was Anne Watson, the sister of Thomas Watson a good friend of mine. Robert told me he liked women, but he enjoyed to punish them, for he saw women as being weak, as his own mother had been. I was never sure how strong Robert's true feelings were. They would write sweet letters to each other and in fact there was one that was quite explicit from Robin. I had that letter and kept it for a long time. I returned it to Robin, at his request, and I kept two others. He thought there had been two more than I gave him, but assumed he had burnt them. I eventually took them with me to the Continent.

Robin had asked for the return of the letters, which would have implicated himself with Anthony, just before the arrests. Robin had offered in one of his letter that he could poison the Earl of Leicester and even the Royal Court. He knew of several ways in which he could poison: gloves; clothes and food, or whatever Anthony thought best he do. I spoke to Robin about this letter and he said that it was part of the ensnarement. "As you know Christopher", he said, when you are an agent of the Queen, to gain a man's confidence who is a traitor, you have to assure him that you are totally on his side and you believe all in he believed in. You are but a courier young Christopher, but soon you will learn the ways of a double-agent, for I am your teacher, so learn well and you will live to a ripe old age.

One evening, Sir Anthony asked me a strange question, I only being a courier, helping the cause. "Do you think Robin loves me well." I couldn't answer that. I turned to him and said: "I think you should ask him that yourself Sir Anthony".

It was not long, about the 4th and 5th of August, arrests were made. They were all picked off one-by-one. Sir Anthony was found several days later hiding in St John's Wood. I was told Sir Anthony said: "Sweet Robin has betrayed me". Sir Anthony couldn't accept that Robin had done such a thing. He was heartbroken. Robin of course was arrested later and sent to the Tower. Once arrested Anthony wrote a letter to his Sweet Robin which I saw. This was the time that he asked if Robin wasn't true to him and didn't love him enough, he was to return his diamond ring and £1,000. Also at the time he sent a petitioning letter to Sir Walter Raleigh with £1,000, which Raleigh kept but did nothing in his favour. I spoke to Raleigh and told him that Sir Anthony didn't deserve to die. Sir Walter turned upon me and said: "All traitor's deserve to die". "You are a bit wet behind the ears boy, don't you be taken in as he is as guity as the rest of them and remember who you serve".

When I visited Robin in the Tower with a letter from Sir Francis, I asked him if he did have any feelings for Sir Anthony and if he did, why did he not save him from torture, by just dispatching him himself. Robert looked at me, with his eyes as cold as ice. "I am not you Christopher, you will have to learn to close your heart. However way you see it, he was a traitor and all traitor's must die a traitor's death. Now leave me." He then turned away from me. Although he spoke these words, all the years I knew Robert he wore that diamond ring on his finger and never once removed it and never spoke the name of Anthony Babington from that day onwards nor have me mention his name any more.

After the arrests Robert Poley was interrogated for two hours and when I saw him he told me "Sir Francis has used me ill". He sat for several hours a day in his cell writing a full report on the Babington Plot, claiming his innocence, and that he was only doing good for his country. Sir Francis had to make an example of him, so he was incarcerated for at least two years, but this didn't mean he was idle, for he gained the confidence of other catholic prisoners, sifting out any information that could be useful and poisoning by order of Sir Francis, those he thought to be dangerous. Although Robert had blown his cover due to the Babington Plot, he started a new career on his release. He took over the running of the spy network in the Low Countries and the Continent. It was then he took me under his wing, to teach me his ways.

Sir Anthony Babington by psychic artist David Calvert-Orange

Alleyway in Middle Row, Dunstable, Bedfordshire.
(Photograph by Neville Harwood)

Chapter 5

Peter Basconi

It was the latter part of the 1580s and I was visiting the Rose theatre. It was here that I saw a youth of about 14 or 15 years old who had temporarily joined the company of players, and he was reading and rehearsing his lines. The play is irrelevant, but there were many being performed then: my 'Jew of Malta'; 'Tamburlaine', which was very popular; 'The Massacre at Paris'; and I was writing 'Henry II' and 'Faustus'. I happened to see the young man as he kept brushing his hair away that allowed me to catch a glimpse of his face. I had never seen such a beautiful young man in my life. You know when you look at someone, this was love at first sight. And this is how I felt for him. I couldn't get his face out of my mind, if you understand me. I must know who he was, so I asked Philip Henslowe who said his name was Peter and he had joined the cast temporarily. He was from the Continent and had been studying over here, and wanted to join the English theatre. So I watched him, for his beauty was befitting to play the womens' parts. He was the epitomy of beauty for such a part. Philip I said: "he must be given the best role". Philip said: "that we could not override the other actors", so I went to speak to Ned Alleyn, Ned agreed with me because the young man being so beautiful would draw an audience. I waited for him, and he didn't really notice me. I followed with the actors to the Anchor on Bankside, close to the Rose, and he was sitting there. I introduced myself, we spoke for a little while, but he seemed quite distant. He put his hand out to me and touched me. Pray do not think me ill-mannered sir but there is much to learn. I felt a shiver through my body… and I knew that he was meant for me. He looked at me, and those eyes … they seemed to draw me in. Nervously, I said that's alright, but do you mind if I just sit here and drink my beer. He replied with a smile: "no, please do". So I did, but I could not take my eyes off this paragon of beauty which held my gaze. His hair an abundance of tawny brown curls which fell beyond his shoulders. He had eyes like sapphires, his nose was slender, and his lips were full and inviting, so hard not to resist planting a kiss upon. A complexion so fair, he hath bewitched me with his beauty. His body shapely in a womanly sense, his hands soft with long fingers and nails polished. He walked with gracefulness and sweetness in his speech… All I wanted to do was just look at him, but decided that I might finish my drink and bid my farewell.

So then I went home, and as I walked along I just could not get him off of my mind. When I returned to my lodgings Will was there and I spoke to him about this young man. He laughed at me and he jested, then said, "Ah, Kit is in love again."

"No, no, no, this is not for plays. This is real."

"Ah yes, we've heard this one before. Oh come on, let's go and get some pasties."

"Ah no, I couldn't eat, I couldn't sleep…"

"Oh, you have got it bad," he said. Then he laughed and said, "Oh don't worry, when you have conquered him you will be feeling better, you know. It won't take long."

I said: "You know what it is like when you fall." He chided me for being so like a schoolboy.

My Truth

I was trying to write and he said: "You know, Henslowe will be wanting a play." And I couldn't write, I couldn't think. My mind was on this beautiful youth. He was so, so goddess-like, too beautiful to be a man.

Eventually I went to bed, but I couldn't sleep, tossed and turned all night. I was restless, sat up in my bed and thought I must get to know this young man. But he avoided me. I felt at first that maybe he was shy and that I needed to wait. But I didn't want to wait too long. I didn't want someone else to take away this paragon of beauty from me. Will kept saying, "Oh don't worry, Give him time." And Robin Poley... Actually he ruined it because in a way he could be a roguish knave, he kept saying, "Oh, if you conquer him, if you bed him, I'll bet you so much." But it wasn't me who made the bet, it was him. And he went and told Peter that it was me. One particular night I went to visit Peter, and waited for him to leave the theatre, I approached, he came forward I thought in friendship. I didn't try to seduce him, yet he attacked me and put his knee to my groin, giving me such pain in my cods. And after he had done this to me he turned and said, "I am not here to be your paramour. I have heard about you and your liaisons, also the way you have treated lovers, so you are not going to use me Mr Marlowe as you have used others." He told me that he knew about the wager and that I had set it. I replied through my pain, "No, I didn't," but he did not want to know. So he left me. Robin thought it was funny, so I was angry with him. He had made it sordid in his wrong way of thinking. Maybe he was a little jealous, I don't know. But I thought no, I am not going to give in to this. Robin said: "Oh well, there are plenty of other men, other boys." But I didn't want other boys, I wanted him, but not for the reasons of the past where I lusted. I knew I was in love with this man. Robin said: "How can you be in love with him when you don't know him?" But I said: "I do know him. I know him like I know myself."

"What about Thomas?" I shall always love him, but we have fell out of love. I am still in love with him, but only at a distance. I will always be there for him, but I am only human. Even you are unable to judge.

Eventually I found out where he was staying. So I went to his lodgings and his landlady showed me where his room was. Up I went and knocked on his door, he opened it then went behind the door to close it, but I held the door open. I said: "That's alright, you can slam the door in my face, you can throw me out, but I want you to listen to what I have to say." He eventually let me in. I put my cards on the table and told him that I had had affairs, yes, and you probably heard about me. He said yes, and that he knew that I and Thomas Walsingham were lovers." "Yes, that was so, but not in the physical sense, not at this moment in time. But he will always be there for I will always love him and that is something you will have to accept." He said he would need time to think it over as he had been hurt in his life too many times, and he didn't want to be hurt again. He did have a lover who had used him cruelly and broke his heart. He felt that he didn't want to go through that pain again. He was not going to be abused again or taken advantage of. That was why he was so angry being treated as if he was some sort of a rent boy." Tears welled up in his eyes. He was not a rent boy, and he was not going to be treated in that manner. He said: "You are not going to bugger me like the others." He then broke down, sobbing like a child. I took his trembling hands and softly said to him: "Peter, I don't do that, I don't like that word and I don't want you to say it again. I make love, I don't do such things and never wish you to ever think of me in this way. I have made mistakes but I will never hurt you, physically or mentally."

He said to me: "I want you to prove to me that if you love me enough you will be with me, but I am not going to give myself to you until I feel I am ready too. And I want you to prove to

My Truth

me that you love me." I lifted his hand to my heart, then my lips and kissed them gently. My promise to you, now please don't weep. I took the kerchief from my poke and dried his tears for him.

So I promised I would be true to him and I would help him when ever he needed me. I never made any demands on him, although it was very dificult as you can understand. But then I had to prove myself. So I introduced him to Tom and Sweet Will. They found him charming. Tom remarked he was a far nicer person than other young men. He was accepted at Scadbury. He was a beautiful young man who could sing, he had a wonderful voice. He could play the lute and dance, and had lots of graces and charms.

I took him one Christmas to Scadbury, having met him in late September, and it was this Christmas that we first kissed each other as lovers, but he then pushed me away. I was angry, and I know I should not have done it, but I pushed him out into the cold. I felt I was being flirted with. He was weeping in the cold outside. I know it was wrong, but I too was hurt. It was cold and he was crying to be let back in, I realised what I was doing, and let him in. I was sorry because he was so cold. So I picked him up and carried him to my room and put him to bed. I said I was very sorry for what I had done and how selfish I was. He said that it was his fault and took himself off to his own chamber, wishing me goodnight. At that moment I thought I had lost him and chided myself for being so bold and what a fool I was. So I lay in the darkness watching the snow falling, until I drifted into sleep.

It was in the middle of the night that I awoke to see Peter stood there in my chamber at the foot of my bed, he said that he would become my lover, but he felt it would be wrong as we were in my former lover's home. I said if he felt uncomfortable, we would wait until we returned home to London. But I reminded him, Thomas and I were friends and not lovers as we had been. And I said that it was up to him, for I did not want to force him. He got into bed with me and I held him close in my arms, as if afraid to let him go, that he may go away again. Then lifted his face up to mine and kissed him tenderly. The passion rose between us and then I made him mine.

He stayed true to me, no matter what I had done. But he didn't know everything about me, although he did eventually. For in time I felt that I had to tell him, but knew he could be trusted. Although I was ten years older than him I discovered that he himself was very mature in his mind. He could write Latin, sing and chant in Latin. He had been well educated. He wouldn't tell me too much about himself, only that his mother was English and his father Italian from Padua. Upon his mother's death he was sent to England to his uncle to further his education. His uncle was not too happy with his nephew in the theatre. So knew he would return back to me at some point.

Peter continued to act, and we became lovers, but I had to keep Peter in the dark about my other dealings than the playmaking, for I did not want harm to become of him. This proved good when sadly Thomas Kydd was implicated a few years later. So when Peter went back to his uncle I was relieved but kept in touch and it was in later years he became my companion and confidant.

I learned to understand this young man. He did not like it when I was angry or violent. But unlike other men who would run away, like Thomas Kydd who was fearful of me, he stood up to me and he wouldn't take any messing. He would put his hands on his hips and stand his ground. I never laid a hand on him. I may have shouted at him, but he wouldn't have it, and he would tell me what he thought of me. And there were times, yes, he was right. But at the time he didn't know what I was going through and what I was doing. Eventually he did

My Truth

find out, for when troubles came I had to be honest with him. But that is when everything fell into place.

I would visit him and spent time together when we could. We used to like to take walks in the woodland and sit by the streams. And we would take some food with us. I loved to be by rivers and in the woodland. I would take paper with me, and the inkhorn, and write. Peter liked to write poetry himself, and he could sketch for he was quite a good artist. He would sketch the woodlands, and he liked to draw people and their expressions. He drew a few of me, but I don't know if they are in existence. We would be together. I would write poems and he would draw pictures to complement the poems. I would write some words to my plays, for he was my muse, my inspiration. He was beauty that spurred me on. In my plays he was this beautiful woman, my beautiful youth. As he grew older his beauty never faltered. He had fine cheekbones and he looked after himself. His skin was always soft and even into his older years you could see how beautiful he had been once. A person ages, but they don't look old. There were times when I often thought why did he put up with me, live with me as you would say in your words. At times I could be angry and frustrated, but he stood by me. And to me that was a true soulmate. I started to tell him about myself one day when we were going for a walk in the country. I told him about my dealings in the Service and the reasons why I went away for long times. He didn't seem surprised. He knew that I must have been doing something of importance. He would give me information from what he heard in the theatre for there were times when he would hear people talking and gossiping. But he knew the difference between gossip and potential information. However, I did not want to involve him or I did not want him harmed. If I was ill Peter would take care of me, but I am afraid I wasn't a very good patient. Peter was patient with me to a degree. You have heard the saying 'Met your match?' This is what it was. He understood that I was in the Service, but he wanted to know why I had got myself involved. I told him that at first I took it on as a courier and then it became exciting, but now I had realised that it was rather dangerous. But I didn't want him to be too involved as I had mentioned. He told me a little about his own family and where he came from, and that his family had helped people from other countries in the past, and that he had connections in Italy. But he liked it in England; he liked the English theatre. He said that in Venice women were on the stage. I was a little appalled about it; I didn't like it myself. But that was just me. We talked an awful lot about my work, my plays and he was a great inspiration for them. We talked of poetry, and I said that I was going to write a poem called 'Hero and Leander'. It is a great legend about two lovers who met in secret, and he would swim the Hellespont to be with her. And Peter said would I swim the river to be with him, and I said yes, I would, and that I would do anything for him. And the thing that I wanted to do was protect him. He said that I had not to worry and that he would be careful. I said that if anything were to happen to myself he was not to get involved and deny all knowledge of me. As far as others were concerned they thought that he was just another boy, another paramour; and this is how we kept it.

We had fun together and so enjoyed each others company. He had an endearing habit with his hair, where he would push it up under a cap so that it didn't hang around his face too much. When Will and I wrote 'A Midsummer Night's Dream' we had Peter in mind when writing of Puck. He could move very quickly, and he could run faster than me too. I remember chasing him, and we were crossing the water on stepping-stones and I missed my footing and fell in. Peter thought it was funny. We had some wonderful times together. I don't like to look on our relationship as being any different to a heterosexual one because if you love someone it doesn't matter. What you do behind closed doors is nothing to do with anyone else. I was happy to live with him as a recluse some years later. He understood me. It was like loving myself loving him, if you understand what I mean. He cared. And when he thought that I was dead Will said that he was so down. I was going to tell him what was going to happen, but because we didn't want to draw attention to events Will said that he would tell him later, and he did. He told him after the funeral. Peter was distraught. Well, almost suicidal, which is why Will said that he had to tell him that I was still alive. But that was all right because then he could come and see me. He could not come right away of course because we were afraid lest anyone followed. So he just came to see me when he could. Will took care of him, made sure he was all right, and he had work obviously. I knew that he was looked after, but between that time he was my inspiration – my muse. Will took letters to him for me.

I was pleased Tom had accepted him, but there was probably an underlying reason because of the other families in Italy, Peter had connections with. Once in Italy I ended up living with Peter as a recluse. A recluse is someone who chooses to live alone, yes? I decided that there was nothing else I could do to change my situation. I did my bit for the Service on the Continent, but you see I lived for my writing. And it was very hard too for those at home. I did come home a few times, and I was trying to get back home permanently. I came over in 1598 for a while, which was when I was ill; and in 1603. You see it was so difficult because my friends were being watched by those who were after what I had in my possession.

Peter Basconi by psychic artist David Calvert-Orange

Chapter 6

The Bradley affray

Methinks the affray happened upon the afternoon in mid-September, upon the way to the Curtain theatre. I was accosted by a Mr William Bradley who was a year or so older than myself. He was the son of an innkeeper, a roguish fellow and a scoundrel to boot. He owed monies all over, but did owe John Alleyn. John's lawyer Hugh Swift was the brother-in-law to Tom Watson. Tom told me that this knave Bradley had made vicious threats to Hugh, so when Tom tried to settle this, Bradley threatened him with great malicious intent.

He was no match for me, for I played with him like a cat and mouse, that was until he started to wear down, but he still kept on. Tom then appeared through the crowd angry and disturbed. It must have angered him so, because he said that he could not take any more. He said: "do not get involved, leave this villain to me, I will deal with him, and I alone". Unfortunately the following day I had no choice, for his problem became my problem too. I remember leaving the house and walking steadily down the lane, when I felt a presence of someone behind me. He placed his sword upon my shoulder. At this point I stopped abruptly and turned, only to be faced with Bradley. He knew that Tom and I were close friends. I recall thinking at that moment maybe one of my enemies had caught up with me. I heard this voice calling me a 'filthy playwright' and other such words of insults. I tried to remain calm. "I have no axe to grind with thee Bradley", I said. He continued to goad me further, until I could take no more of it. Having hold of my sword by its hilt and on my guard, I withdrew it and said: "you wish to cross swords?"

We fought down the lane and a crowd started to gather round. Then among them came Tom who tried desperately to pull me out of there. It was no use though; Bradley kept on coming towards me, lunging at me with his sword. I had no choice but to keep on going, first using my sword and then parrying with my dagger.

Tom realising what had happened, intervened and pushed me out of the way. I stumbled and fell heavily upon the ground. Tom continued to fight with him. They had gone but only a few yards when I heard a loud scream. Struggling to my feet I went over to where they were. Thinking first it was Tom, but alas, it was Bradley lying there slain who had died from the wounds. Tom had been injured in the stomach and in his left hand, but thankfully he was still alive, for the wound was not too deep a cut.

Tom never really recovered from what happened that day. In fact it was but a few years further on that Tom passed as a result of the fight and of course the ill treatment he received whilst in Newgate prison. I was bitterly disappointed for not being at his side when he died. I was away on foreign shores and it was not until my return I heard of this sad news. I dedicated a poem in his memory, for he had been a good and loyal friend and one of the finest poets among us.

We were arrested and taken in custody by the constables, then taken to prison at Newgate. The arresting officer by the name of Wylde, was a tailor. He had us both manacled and pushed in a hole of foul stench called limbo and all we had for light was one single candle, which stood on a black rock known as the Black Dog of Newgate. The floor was wet with piss and other such body waste that filled our nostrils. Tom vomited several times as I did too. There were rats that scratched beneath our feet. I kicked several of them away. If there was a hell, this was it. You could hear the screams and moans of the other inmates. Upon first light the following day we were acquitted and given a verdict of self-defence on both counts. My bail was to be arranged but Tom had to wait until February before he was released. Two gentlemen who were acquaintances of Tom paid my bail, so I was soon out of there. Monies and help were sent to Tom to ease his incarceration, also his wounds were dressed and he was given clean linen.

I shall never forget the stench. The horror of men crying, the shear blackness and the morbid fear of never again seeing the light of day. It took weeks for me to get the smell of that stench from out my nostrils. I burned the clothes; it was the only way the odour was able to go away, for no amount of washing would clear it.

It was at that time our bond as friends became ever closer than before, for we kept each other sane, Thomas was a true friend and mentor, he guided me through my literary works, giving me good counsel. He stood by me in word and deed. I hated leaving him in that hellhole of a prison.

His passing left a void in my life and I knew, though he wasn't here in the flesh to guide me, he was there when I needed him, to inspire me in my work. Never, ever did I forget him. I recall Ned giving me the news, the heart within my breast sank, for I could not withhold the tears, the grief was too much for me to bear. Thomas you will live forever a sweet friend, always in my thoughts, that is until the day I have breathed my last.

The incident troubled me for sometime. So much so, I oft times wondered whether or not I could have caught Tom in his side and it was through this he became ill and passed away.

Chapter 7
Living with Thomas Kydd

Not long after coming to London I met another Tom, Thomas Kydd. He was quiet, reserve, and a lonely young man. He was a poet and playwright like myself. His parents were staunch churchgoers. His father a scrivener of the Law Courts and his mother, Agnes I believe her name was. I recall that in our conversations his mother figured more prominently than his father. Maybe this was because he treated him cruelly.

I can remember my first meeting with Thomas. We were at the Anchor Inn on Bankside, sitting in the corner. The corner was dark, and he was sat at a table with a jug of ale in his hand appearing to be deep in thought. I had seen him before in the inn, looking as if he was carrying the whole world upon his shoulders, so I went over to speak to him and asked him if he would like to take 'sup' and 'salt' (meaning: to eat with me). He presently accepted and we began to talk in a friendly manner, as if we had always been friends. Thomas Watson said I must have been honoured to have him speak with me, for he was not one who would make conversation nor mix well in company.

We started to make much conversation and became good friends. Eventually I decided to move in with him at his lodgings. But before I made this decision we often discussed our plays and poetry together. When he was completing his Spanish Tragedy he asked my advice, I told him that it was an excellent play full of fire and passion. He said that he wanted to write poetry. I oft times listened to what he wrote and gave advice when it was warranted. Although I was a University man – a 'university wit' – as I was known, I never condemned another fellow writer because of his lack of University teaching. Just because you never entered university, it did not mean you were unable to write. Often though other playwrights condemned him because of this. They said he should stick to what he was, a scrivener meaning noverint, but I thought this most unfair.

I don't know how you think, but if a man is capable of writing, why should he not write? I would give him the benefit of my knowledge and learn the benefit of his. He would copy out some of my work because my handwriting was not always very legible, because I had to get everything down while it was in my head. Tom had very beautiful handwriting that was clear to read.

Thomas Kydd was helping me with my plays including Titus Andronicus, which Thomas Kydd I'm sure would want to take the credit for, as it was mostly his. At the time he was also working on Hamlet and a play called A Midsummer Night's Dream – an idea of mine, of which both Will Shakespeare and Thomas had a hand in too. He wrote a poem for me, called 'The Morning Star'. For it was in the School of Night that I was known as this. There were also other pieces of poetry he wrote but he gave no name to them.

Thomas Kydd was taller than I. His hair was flaxen in colour, swept back and a little wavy, but much thicker than mine at the forehead. He had a fair complexion with a moustache, slate grey eyes that used to shine when he was happy.

He was quite sombre in dress and wore brown velvet or black with cream lace. Around his neck he had a chain with a ring on it. He was fairly slim in body but broad on his shoulders, with a slender waist but very sturdy legs and had long slim fingers. He had very graceful manners and wasn't taken to drink, unlike myself, for he only drank what he needed. Very orderly in his room, especially his quills, and he always had large stacks of various papers for the work that he was doing.

As I previously mentioned, like his father, he was a 'scrivener'. He copied documents and was a secretary. Employed by Lord Strange to write plays and do secretarial work for him. Lord Strange was a suspected secret catholic, who I later had to spy upon. Something that Thomas was afeared of, as he had many powerful connections, Lord Strange that is.

Thomas knew nothing of my spying and he never enquired, as he kept his thoughts to himself.

There were those who thought him jealous of me, but so too were many others. He once said that God had given me so many gifts but I flouted them, and why had he not been blessed in the same way. Many times he said he could not help but love me, even though I'd lied to him. Some years later after he was tortured, he confessed that he wrote much anger about me, half of it being true.

We were lovers admittedly, but looking back I should never have allowed the relationship to develop. I never really meant for it to be serious, but somehow Thomas wanted more. I remember it was at Yuletide, and some years later, when I was in exile, I can recall reflecting upon my relationship with him. The winter I speak of was back in 1589, when first I went to reside with Thomas; his lodgings were not too far away from St Paul's churchyard.

Thomas Kydd's rooms were spacious. There was a small chamber with a cooking pot over the fire, cupboards for preserves, platters and bowls, a table and two chairs. On the table stood two candlesticks, and a box for holding spoons and knives. The window was small, over which hung a blue slightly faded curtain. The floorboards were well scrubbed and sprinkled with rushes (daily). The writing chamber, as Thomas would call it, was larger with a fireplace and a wooden mantle. On it stood three wood and pewter candlesticks. Each side of the fireplace there were two shelves. To the left of the fireplace, nearest to the window, stood a large oak chest for books and papers. In front of this stood an old, but highly polished oak table with two sturdy chairs either side. Upon the table stood an inkstand, a long wooden box containing several quills, and beside the box lay a silver-handled penknife. On the smaller table in the corner of the room were two bottles of wine, and four pewter goblets, beside the fireplace stood a two-seater settle upon which were two large blue cushions made of the same fabric as the curtains in both rooms. The floor was stained and polished with a few scented rushes.

In the bedchamber was a large oak four-poster bed with roses carved on the back panel; linen upon it was white and crisp. The coverlet and hangings were of dark green velvet with matching curtains at the window, a gift from his parents. At the side of the bed was also a small table that had on it a candlestick and at the foot was a large chest. The fireplace in the room was similar to that of the other room. On top of its mantelpiece were two pewter candlesticks. Directly to the left of the fireplace near the window was a washstand and on it were a looking glass, pitcher and bowl. At the side of the stand was another stand, which had fresh towels on it. Stood at the corner of the fireplace was a chair on which was draped some clothes and nearby was a smaller chest. The wooden floor was scattered with scented rushes.

I recall our first Yuletide together; it was a very happy occasion. Thomas decorated our lodgings with holly and mistletoe and put some mistletoe in our bedchamber. It was Yuletide Eve; I was working on my play 'The Jew of Malta'.

My Truth

Thomas came home around six of the clock – myself being so deep in thought – I did not hear him enter, until I felt his arms firmly around my shoulders. I recall him asking "How has thou fared in thy playmaking today Kit?" I turned to face him. "Well Thomas I have managed to draw up the first draft of my play. Would you like to peruse it?" Thomas took the papers from my hand and put them back on the table. "First things first Kit, have you eaten today?" I bowed my head and told him "nay I have not, not since breaking my fast this morning." "Well all is well Kit, we have a goose for dinner on the morrow and being as you've kept both fires burning, you can fetch my cloak from the bedchamber and we will be away to the inn to down a couple of flagons of mulled ale before having our supper." I protested, "but Thomas, you know that I have promised Edward Alleyn a new play, for which he has already paid me two pounds in advance". Before I could finish talking Thomas had brought my cloak, throwing it around my shoulders and pulling me from out of the chair. "Come on Kit he said, we are going out for a while and that is that, no arguments." So off we went.

When we got to the inn it was very full, there were people pushing and shoving and calling out for service. Thomas and I found a nice spot by a welcoming fire. One of the serving wenches came over to us. "Well now if it isn't Mr Marlowe and Mr Kydd what is your pleasure?' I smiled at her and said 'a couple of flagons of your best ale." She then hurried herself away, no sooner had she gone she came hurrying back, putting the flagons down on the table and said, and "these are on the house". Thomas raised his tankard saying, "let us drink to our health", he then turned to me and said, "Well Kit, will thou be coming with me to Midnight Mass?" I paused for a moment. "You know how I feel about the Church Thomas." "But 'tis only my Parish Church of St Mary's, Kit. Both my parents will be there, my brother and my sister too. Please come, if only for me" I took my last swallow of ale and replied, "I will think about it between now and supper". Thomas finished his drink, and then we had a couple more drinks before going back to our lodgings.

When we got back we hurriedly took off our cloaks and sat in front of the warm fire. "Next year Thomas, I am going to work much harder at my play making and poetry. "Yes, it's what you were born to do, don't waste your life. It's not worth it Christopher, for they will ruin you, use you, leaving you to die like a beggar" those who would have you think are your friends. I never realised that Thomas was so concerned and would chance to speak out in this way. "Thomas Walsingham has promised me that no harm will come to me or my friends." "It is not Thomas Walsingham I distrust, for I know that he honours his word, 'tis the others, you know the ones I am referring to Christopher." Thomas rose to his feet abruptly and walked across the room to the window, unlocking it and letting in the night air. I followed him, his hand resting upon the windowsill. I gently placed my hand over his and to my amazement felt it trembling. He turned to face me, and I could see in his eyes a mixture of love and envy. He pushed my hand away saying: "You share my lodgings and my bed yet your heart is elsewhere, why is this?" It was from that moment I discovered the true feelings he had for me. A silence was then broken by Thomas, "forgive me Christopher, 'tis no business of mine, you have your own life to lead dost thou not", I then moved towards him. "Thomas, I understand that thou hast feelings for me (but I must confess not before this night) please come and sit beside me and finish your drink." This he did, but I knew what Thomas felt for me was deeper than just a friendly concern. He asked me again if I would like to go with him to Midnight Mass, but I declined. "It is better that I do not, for it would be wrong of a me and hypocritical." Without more ado Thomas nodded to me and left our lodgings. Not having the heart for writing I placed some more logs on the fire and returned to the settle. I must

My Truth

have dozed off in front of the fire, for the next thing I heard was Thomas speaking to me, "Kit, wake up, 'tis Yuletide."

We collaborated on many of the works. He then began work on another play based upon the Prince of Denmark that I mentioned before. We would both sit and meditate, allowing our inspiration to flow. Thomas loved the springtime when the flowers were coming into bud for he was very fond of primroses. He liked the pond lilies and lilac trees nearby with their sweet scented fragrance.

There were many about who were very jealous and envious of me, but on the other hand there were those who had much admiration for me too. I recall Thomas saying that he was much gladdened for knowing me. After lodging with Thomas I started to write a poem based on the Greek legend of 'Hero and Leander' in the Yuletide of 1592. George Chapman, a fellow poet and friend, completed the poem for me, but it was not to my taste, for I would not have written it in the same vain.

Thinking on poor Thomas Kydd, he was innocent on all what was to come and I am very sorry for what befell him and I want those who read this book to know this. What he said in anger and mixed with fear, there was some truth. We parted company writing and sharing lodgings together, for this strained our friendship, he wanted more from me, but my feelings were not of lover or of a lover, only a friend. He wanted more than I could give. Like he said many times, my heart was elsewhere. So he moved on and I moved out. We still remained friends although a little difficult at times. He did not deserve the ill way he was treated and his life ruined, so in the end he took his own life, upon believing he was the cause of my death.

Chapter 8
Robert Poley

Of all the men in my life, there was one who through the years I had kept company, he was Robert Poley. We first met as I may have mentioned, in the year of our Lord 1585. A man once met never forgotten.

He was about ten years or so my elder, we were of similar height although he was slimmer in build and much more muscular. He had a fair complexion with shoulder length golden hair and his beard and moustache much straight, was tinged with red. His eyes could allure you and yet could turn you to ice; they were blue and clear. He had a manner to the manor-born, well bred and educated, for he had studied at Claire College, Cambridge. He was immaculate in every way, his moustache and beard were always neatly trimmed, hair combed and nails clean and well manicured. He would dress sombrely but they were always well-tailored clothes. He mostly favoured red or claret, for he once mad a quip that blood did not show up so easily on these.

When we were in close conversation he mentioned that while at university he was a sizar, which meant he had to earn his keep, he paid nothing for food and tuition, and not much for his lodgings. He ran errands for the more wealthy students, made their beds, emptied the piss-pots and laid their table and other such menial tasks. He even played bedfellow to those who favoured him. At first he was angry, but turned it to his own advantage and made himself a pretty penny into the bargain, 100 pounds or more at the time he left.

He told me that his father died after a long illness when he was but ten years of age, but leaving his mother, a younger brother and himself comfortably off. There was money put aside for him to go to university, but alas his mother re-married unwisely. His stepfather was not a cruel man, but sadly made bad investments. His mother loaned him the money put aside for Robert, which was lost and what other monies were needed for the maintenance in the hard months ahead. He told me that he could never forgive his mother for being so foolish. I asked him if he gained his degree, he never answered the question, for it was a sore point, so I never pursued it again.

He was married, but left his wife Anne, sister to Thomas Watson the poet and friend of mine, not long after their daughter Anne was born. His marriage was falling apart, so he thought it best to leave his wife and baby daughter. It was after his daughter's birth his wife became strange and found her hard to live with even though he employed a maid to help her, he realised that he didn't love her after all. That was not to say that he had no love for his daughter and he always made sure that she was provided for. To get him out of this situation he told me that he pleaded with Mr Secretary to put him in the Marshalsea under a trumped-up charge, so that he could spy on catholic prisoners there. He said that his wife came there every day pleading with the gaoler to see him but Robert said he refused her admittance.

He met another woman, Joan Yeoman while in the Marshalsea; moderately wealthy as she was wife of a cutler. Robert told me that she was pretty but not overly bright, just how he liked them and married and that situation suited him well.

After leaving the Marshalsea he then went to lodge with his mistress and her husband, causing rather a lot of unrest between them. In the end he told me that she ran away with him, but in later years that she returned to her husband. Not long after this, the woman gave birth to a son of which Robert always insisted he was the father.

Robert never stayed too long with a woman. It was not so much that he grew tired of them, but the hate he had for his mother, therefore he thought all women were foolish and silly and he always chose women of such nature and married. Always a safe wager, he said, but with his own sex that was an entirely different matter. I once asked him if he did love Anthony Babington, "no" was his curt reply. He was a little like the women in my life, "silly vain and foolish". Robert I said, "Anthony Babington was besotted with you, and believed in you". Robert's reply was, "more the fool him" and he spoke no more on the matter.

As I recall, when I visited him in the Tower of London just before Anthony Babington's execution, Robert appeared to be weeping. Although I never questioned it, this showed to me that he was human and that he really did have feelings, but suppressed it.

When he was schooling me in the ways of intelligence, he instilled into me that you closed your heart and used your head, kept your wits about you, kill or be killed. Robert told me, "there is no sentiment in the game my friend, there may come a time when I may have to despatch you or you me. When interrogated you tell them nothing, only what you want them to know".

This man 'sweet Robin', as he was known, was a roguish knave, a liar, and a forger and was even accused of treachery, but I being fully aware accepted him for what he was. Yes, I slept with him as a lover and my first encounter was in the early years. I was passing through Dunstable at the time, unaware that he had followed me, for he wished to know if Anthony Babington had given me anything he should know about.

It was late evening and I was passing through an alleyway, I could see a silhouette in the darkness. As this figure walked towards me I recognised him. He put his arm out to block my way and in a quiet voice, "hello Christopher, I thought I'd missed you". "I've been on business," I replied. I know, he replied, "mission accomplished?" I nodded, "yes". "That's good, but I haven't come to see you about that. Shall we retire to that inn over there, I need to speak with you in private." Linking his arm with mine, "let's hurry along then, I am also very hungry". He requested a room at the back of the inn and our supper brought up. We both ate and drank in silence and in the silence I could sense something was amiss. When all was cleared away Robert then broke the silence. "I think you know why I'm here?" "No, I replied", he then banged his fist on the table. "Don't play the innocent with me." "Did Anthony give you a package for me or a token?" "No, I replied," the package was hidden at my lodgings under the floor, the other was on my person, but I thought I had discarded it. Robert grabbed my arm and pushed me against the wall. "You do have something," so give it to me now or you will not only endanger your life but mine too. "Alright let's take some air," put your cloak on and we'll walk back to the alley. "Now I could kill you here, but as you belong to me …". "I belong to no one", I replied." "That's what you think Christopher Marlowe," his hand on his dagger … "you have one minute." His eyes seemed to flash in the darkness of the alley. I was frozen to the spot. I reached into my doublet and before I could hand it to him, he snatched it from my grasp. I could see by his face in the moonlight that he knew by its feel, what it was. "You stay where you are, I shall be back presently." I waited for his return and when he came back he spoke not one word on our return to the inn.

When the door to our room was closed and bolted he then spoke, "are you sure he gave you nothing else?" "Yes, was my reply, I thought it was just a brooch but one that could have implicated both of us Robert." It belonged to Mary Queen of Scots, a token that she gave to those who were loyal to her cause. "Christopher you must learn to trust me, for I am your master, second to Sir Francis. You must never speak abroad about what has happened this night, promise me this." "I paused for a moment... yes, I promise you nothing will be spoken, and I give you my word on it." With this I gave him my hand, which he took. "I promise". Robert said, "your hand is cold, you have nothing to fear so long as you follow my advice." His eyes met mine and there was warmth as he drew me towards him, putting his other arm around my shoulder no words were spoken, his lips were on mine and then passion within both us became stronger. He put his tongue inside my mouth and mine in his. Our hands fumbling to undo each other's clothes and leaving them in disarray upon the floor as we made our way towards the bed, both our naked bodies lay naked in the candle glow. We caressed and fondled each other and explored each other's bodies before kissing him on his lips again. I started to suck on his nipples, which seem to arouse the passion more within him, before moving down to his belly, and at this point he was becoming more aroused. I then took his aroused prick between my moistened lips and gently played with my tongue until his sweet nectar flowed forth. Already aroused myself, I took sweet Robin, entering him in a loving embrace. When all our passion was spent, we both fell into slumber wrapped in each other's arms.

The following dawn I awoke to find Robin Poley gone. He left me a note, telling me that the bill had been paid and with the note was a pouch of money and a silver posy ring, which I placed on my finger. On the ring was an inscription in Latin, but the words escape me at this moment.

Over the years I worked with him on the continent, the Low Countries and before my exile. I went with him on several occasions to Scotland, taking despatches to King James VI. Robert knew Scotland well and knew the safe route into there, as it was not an easy place to travel through, but with the right knowledge and contacts you were able to do this safely. On one occasion Robert confided in me on his dealings and that he would impart knowledge that I had to swear on oath that I would repeat to no other, this to keep silent. He told me that he had made a fair profit in his double-dealings, which was taking payment from the Catholics and Mr Secretary. The only reason he told me this was because he felt he could trust me. He said I could take the money to the continent to give to various contacts. I asked if he was planning to leave the country, he replied, "maybe Christopher, who knows, the money is to be put into lands". The incident at Flushing was connected to Robert and it was Richard Baines, who uncovered our scam and blew my cover into the bargain and his too, with his blabbing to the Authorities. Fortunately Robert spoke to Lord Burleigh and convinced him that he had instructed me to uncover any forgers in the Low Countries. I found the whole matter distasteful. One thing which I will tell thee all in my next part, is the tale of the Meonia, something I learned about from Robert Poley and Anthony Babington for this interested me much. It was infinitely more than just a jewel in a velvet pouch, for it was something of great importance in esoteric matters.

Robert Poley by psychic artist David Calvert-Orange

Chapter 9

Sir Walter Raleigh

Thomas Walsingham first introduced me to Sir Walter at Court as a poet and playmaker. He thought maybe Sir Walter would become my patron too, for he had many influential friends such as Henry Percy, 9th Earl of Northumberland, and the famous mathematician Thomas Hariot. Early the following year I was asked to spy upon Walter when he was in England. His friend Henry Percy came from a staunch Catholic background with an even stronger claim to the English throne than that of James VI of Scotland, also asked to further investigate the rumours put abroad about Walter being an atheist, to discover whether or not they were true.

Thomas told me those at Court were not very fond of him; in fact, they didn't like him at all. In Court circles he was known as the 'most hated man in England'. They said he was arrogant and too self-seeking and they were most concerned about his irreligious views. He was suspected of being an atheist and cared not what people thought of him. A plain-speaking man with a soft cultivated Devonshire accent, which, aggravated the Court even more so. His charm could at oftimes quickly turn to anger, very much like myself. I remember once speaking of the Earl of Essex at Court to Sir Walter and he directly cut me dead. I will not have his name mentioned in my presence, do you understand? After that I did not utter his name lest it would anger him.

My first glimpse of him was when he visited Cambridge. He was riding on horseback, sporting all his finery, but in later years when we two became acquainted, he was a different man entirely, although I was spying on him, I found him to be an interesting and learned man.

As our friendship blossomed, Walter and I found we became kindred spirits in our thoughts of philosophy and like him, I too; questioned the scriptures. I spent many a long hour alone with him in his private chamber in Durham House, and discovered him to be a different man beneath from that you would see at Court.

We talked on many interesting subjects, which would be considered blasphemous. He believed that the elements played a major part on man's existence. His friend Henry Percy was researching the possibility whether magic did work or was it some other phenomenon. Walter held the belief that herbal medicines could assist in curing many ailments. In fact he was noted for making special tonic wines and cordials. One of his many dreams was to make life easier for sailors travelling the high seas, allowing them to drink fresh water, but I do not know if he was successful or not, for when I left, the contact with him ceased. I would only hear snippets of gossip from Thomas in his letters or what was said in the letters from Will, but there was no mention of this, or if he has succeeded or not.

Walter had travelled to the Americas, lived and spoke with the indigenous people, the native American Indians. It was there that he gathered much knowledge and wisdom from their folklore and customs. He said that he was going to write a book on his experiences with these savages. His greatest passion was to discover and rediscover the 'Lost City of Gold', Eldorado, which was south of the Americas. I heard in later

My Truth

years, after my supposed death, that he had discovered it, but I don't know if he ever revealed the truth to anyone else. People believed that he was searching for riches but that was not the whole truth, as he was also searching for hidden knowledge. I discovered a side of Walter that neither the Queen nor his wife ever knew.

I never once thought that he and I would become lovers. I remember it as if it was yesterday, for how can one forget such a meeting. I was visiting him at his London home at Durham House. Nathan, one of his secretary's ushered me into Walter's private study. He was sitting on a settle by the fire. Dressed in a pure silk shirt that hung loosely over his scarlet red velvet knee breeches. He had no stockings on and was wearing a pair of soft black leather slippers. Resting his back against a brightly coloured satin cushion, smoking a long clay pipe. He did not appear to be aware of my presence, his mind being elsewhere.

The room was of a moderate size, with a large bookcase either side of the fireplace. The rest of the walls were of dark oak panelled wainscoting. Over the chimney breast hung a painting of a lake that was surrounded by trees in the moonlight. I thought it an excellent piece of art because the artist had captured the moon's reflection upon the lake. In the window stood a desk, upon it were many papers, a wooden candlestick, double inkstand and pot that held quills, and there were various drawing instruments too. Each side of the desk were two high-backed chairs. In one corner of the room stood a celestial globe, and in the opposite corner there was a globe of the world. A Persian rug was placed in the centre of the polished wooden floor; on it was a pattern of suns, moons and stars that had the most beautiful azure blue background. At the back of the room was a finely carved day bed covered with many large cushions from the Orient. Scattered here and there were low wooden stools, which were padded in the most luxurious blue velvet. Opposite to Walter was another settle with cushions scattered upon it. By the side of the settle where Walter was sitting there was a small round table. On this table was a square wooden box, beside it stood a stand that held various tobacco pipes.

After a short while Walter noticed my presence. "Kit my dear friend," he said in his broad Devonshire accent. He rose from his seat and embraced me as if neither of us had seen each other for some time. There was always warmth whenever he held me close to his breast, but unaware at this time in our friendship, I was unsure of Walter's feelings towards me. But what I was sure of, was my feelings towards him, especially the more times we spent together in each other's company. As time went on it grew harder for me to keep my emotions under control.

"Well Kit, what has the day brought for you then?" I took one of the stools and sat down in front of him. "There is not much to tell Walter. I picked up my quill to write this day, but alas, not even a word would come." Walter then sat back, folded his arms and gave off a sigh. "Well, there's a surprise, our finest poet and playmaker lost for words. Who's the pretty boy or gentleman that is keeping your mind off your writing then? Come on Kit, you tell me."

I paused for a while, what could I do, he had me cornered. I certainly didn't wish for it to go this far. How could I possibly speak the truth, that I was here on business for Mr Secretary, Robert Cecil who had no care or feelings, he just wanted information on Walter and cared not how it was obtained. Meanwhile Walter by this time was growing impatient. "Well, have you lost your tongue, as well as your inspiration?" He smiled and leant over to the small round table beside him, opened the wooden box, then took one of the pipes from his stand and filled it with tobacco from the box. He then rose from his seat and walked over to the fireplace, took a taper from a pot on the mantel and lit his pipe. His pipe in his hand, he walked over to where I was sitting. Handing the pipe to me he said, "here, try this Kit, it will calm your mind my lad." I then took hold of it and started to draw on the weed, but I fear it was too much for my lungs, as I suddenly had a bout of coughing. This amused my host. "No Kit, you must draw upon it slowly, there's plenty of time. Tobacco smoking is an art my lad, observe me." I did has he said and found that it was most helpful. Instead I felt a 'calm' over all of my being. Just then Walter beckoned me to sit beside him. "Come on Kit you will feel more relaxed sat beside me." We sat together smoking our pipes and after we had finished Walter asked me once again the question previously. I remember being afraid to answer, for fear of losing him. Then I blurted it out. "I have fallen for this man, 'tis a gentleman Sir to be precise." There was a silence, and then Walter spoke. "Does he know thee Kit?" "I think so, yes, yes [stumbling over my words] that he does." "Maybe Kit I could put a good word in his ear for thee." I then jumped up from my seat and walked towards the window. "No, [I said abruptly] don't do that Walter, then decided it was time for me to leave, before making a total fool of myself. Then before I could speak, Walter's words came. "It's me, isn't it Kit?" At that instant I made for the door, but Walter quickly rose from his seat and blocked my exit. "I must leave Walter, please let me pass," but he would not. He looked straight at me and said again, "it's me isn't Kit, I am the one you have the love for". I tried desperately to avoid his gaze, but it was no use. We both stood there in the silence, transfixed in one another's gaze. He lifted my chin to face him and repeated what he had said. In almost a whisper I said "yes". Walter then spoke: "I remember the poem you once wrote for me, it was 'The Passionate Shepherd to His Love', of which I wrote the Nymphs reply." "I love you Walter, please forgive me for my boldness, for if you do not feel the same for me, please do not let it stand in the way of our friendship." "What is there to forgive Kit?" Then with those words he took my then trembling hands and drew me towards him. I was now in the arms of the Queen's Favourite and before the evening was over I was lying with him in his bed.

We laid between the silken sheets, in each other's arms, exchanging kisses and caresses. "Take me Walter, I want to feel you inside me, filling me with your love." I recall our bodies and souls becoming 'as one'. Our passion spent, we laid there, two naked lovers in the moonlight. "Kit, what has happened between us this night must not be spoken of abroad and any other times that is to follow must remain sacred?" I stroked his hair and said, "these moments we share I will always treasure". We then drifted into slumber.

At dawn we both awoke, and Walter ushered me out of the house. It was as if nothing had happened between us, but I knew different. He said that he would explain his reasons later.

As I walked through the gardens I could see the tobacco leaves drying, which Walter had brought back from the Americas and the New World. I remember in the School of Night we would use the 'peace pipe' he was given. There were potent herbs mixed in with the tobacco that allowed us to heighten our awareness.

Over time Walter and I became more than just friends. As I mentioned earlier, it was not my intention to become more than just friends, but circumstances changed. Although I did not see him in privy very often, there were times I wished I could have done. His character fascinated me; he was a man of vast knowledge on many things, such as exploring, sea faring, herbalism, history, philosophy, science, law and 'hidden' knowledge.

He visited the theatre to see my plays performed. On one occasion after watching Tamburlaine, Walter was angry with me. In Tamburlaine there is a scene where the virgins are massacred, even though they begged for mercy. Walter said that I was alluding to the massacre in Ireland when he was out there some years before. I replied, "yes, that's right", for I could not understand why he had to kill innocent women and children. He of course denied it, saying that the decision was not left with him, he was following orders and that I keep out of politics.

Walter spoke freely of his views. He said that one should have freedom of speech and be allowed to practise one's own beliefs. And if they so wished, should be allowed to experiment spiritually and scientifically. He believed that man should come out of the Dark Ages. He was sure that many people felt the world was still flat. He did not believe in burning people to the stake nor did he believe in hell. Hell he said was here. Man should progress and stop living in fear. He often talked about the native Indians of the Americas. They lived a peaceful existence, a kind of life he would have exchanged for many times. A man of noble birth, his father being a country squire, but he decided to set out on his own and earn his credibility. Both he and Thomas Hariot went out to the Americas with the sole intent to educate the Indians in the way of Christianity, but ended up instead learning their culture. He respected their teachings and wisdom, for he felt what they had was far better than the Church could offer, but sadly the Church won.

In secret, he wanted the country to be a Republic, something he mentioned to me oftimes. I asked him if the Queen would be put in danger, he assured me that he loved her no matter what had gone before, and no harm would befall her. A short while after the Queen's death he made plans along with Thomas Walsingham (Francis' cousin) to place Arabella Stuart on the throne. I remember agreeing with Walter that it would be in the best interests of the country for it to become a Republic. It would certainly stop the so-called 'hangers-on' bleeding our country dry, but as you know, it is a treasonable offence to go against the government, punishable by death.

There was a plot being put together between Thomas Walsingham and others including Sir Walter, to overthrow the government and take control. The country would then become a Republic like Venice. There was more that I discovered about Walter, but I decided to protect Thomas at all costs, for there were times in later years I felt that I was being used by Walter for his own ends. For it was said that Walter hated my way of life. So why did he lie with me in such a manner. Methinks he may have suspected my dealings, and me, but I shall never know the truth.

Sir Walter Raleigh by psychic artist Denise Bond

Chapter 10

Thomas Walsingham and Scathebury

Thomas Walsingham was cousin to the 'Spymaster' Sir Francis. He and I met briefly at Thomas Watson's home, but our first meeting was at Rye in Sussex. I was instructed to carry a package to him in exchange for another.

I remember there was a chill and the mist was coming up from the sea. I was standing there at the quayside with a cloak pulled well around my shoulders when in the mist I could make out a shape and heard the sound of heavy footsteps as the figure came nearer to me. I recognised Thomas. "Am I glad to see you, I said for it's been so cold waiting for you here, I have almost froze my cods off." Thomas asked if I had been here long, "no" was my reply. Come follow me young man, there's an inn nearby that I know well where we can get a hot meal and a welcoming hearth. We soon did this and got a bed for the night. He asked me how my studies were going and had I written any more poetry or plays. I told him with great excitement that I had started Tamburlaine, the play I spoke of to Thomas Watson. "He's an amazing man old Tom Watson is he not." "Oh he is", I replied and 'tis he who has spurred me on with my plays, for I never thought for one moment that I could be a playmaker. "Well," Thomas said, when it's finished take it around the theatres and see what happens, you have as good a chance as the others. Take it to a budding actor Edward Alleyn, he's looking for the right kind of plays to suit him and I am sure Tamburlaine would suit him down to the ground.

When we retired to our room it was there I gave Thomas the package, he then handed me a letter. I was told to collect a package, Thomas replies, "this letter will explain all", just hand it to my cousin, not Robin Poley and leave it at that, for it's not your worry. "We must get together some time in the near future, Mr Marlowe, or may I call you Christopher?" "Yes, or you can call me Kit." "No", was his sudden reply, "I prefer the name Christopher" and I said, "I prefer Thomas not Tom". Thomas said we both had to be up before the crack of dawn, so we'd best get some sleep. The next thing I remember was Thomas shaking me from my slumber and it was time for me to wake up. I splashed some cold water on my face and got my clothes on and went downstairs to break my fast. Thomas said, "eat up my friend for we must be gone from here soon. I am sure you will find an inn on your way back, but what ever you do, see that my cousin gets the letter personally." I promised him faithfully that I would. Before we rode our separate ways he smiled at me and said quietly, "see you in London Christopher".

I watched him ride off into the distance until I could see him no more. In my heart I knew that there would be many such meetings and a lifetime of commitment, but in what way I did not know. As time moved on all became clear and I would have to give up all my freedom to save this man and those connected with him.

I first visited Thomas' home in Chislehurst, Kent after we had worked on the Babington Plot 1586–87. He had a brother Edmond, many years older than he, he was nothing like Thomas, a pale, thin and sickly man. Thomas complained how he'd allowed the old manor house to be neglected and overgrown in parts.

Thomas was a little older than myself, slightly taller but much slimmer in body, he had light brown hair to his shoulders with a curl in it here and there. His eyes were grey and a small neatly trimmed moustache. He was vain about his looks and you could see his family resemblance to Sir Francis, but this was more apparent in Edmond. Edmond upon my visit greeted me warmly with an apology that he needed to rest and would not be joining us at mealtimes, for he had estate business to attend to and did not wish to be disturbed. He said, "as you are a friend of Thomas, you are welcome to stay as long as you wish".

That evening Thomas and I dined in a small room as he felt it would be much warmer than the great hall. After we had our meal and we were drinking wine Thomas leant across the table putting a hand on my wrist, smiling, he said: "Christopher I know the house is in a shambles, but I shall prove to you on the morrow that his heaven on earth, if you need peace to write my friend, you have found it here." "Before we break our fast I shall take you on a walk." "I look forward to it, but I am afraid you may have to drag me from my bed for I have got into a bad habit of laying late these days." He just smiled and said that my chamber had been prepared next to his, although the building was shabby, but the servants managed to keep the rooms clean.

The following morning both Thomas and I went for a walk through the woodland, the sun was just beginning to stream through the branches on the trees and leaves on them were starting to turn red and gold. We kicked our way through the leaves and Thomas showed me his hiding place when he was a child. He said that he was sure that there was a fairy ring around these parts that had hidden powers in this part of the woods. He also warned me, as his father did to him, to take care in some parts of the estate, as there was danger that the earth would suck you in causing many to disappear. Thomas mentioned there was a cave leading out to other parts of the estate and said in time we will go to it. After he mentioned this a sudden chill went through me and I was overcome with a sense of hidden power. Thomas said: "We will call it Merlin's Cave, for you told me that you are from the Merlin Race, so this is to your cave." When we got back from the woods we had a fine breakfast laid out for us.

In those few days I began to realise that I was in love with this man, but I needed to be sure that he was of the same persuasion as myself. It was at my next visit to Scathebury I discovered that he had the same feelings for me. It was in our secret place in the woods we became lovers, but I always felt that one day I would be taken away from him, so every moment was to be held dear.

Sadly, Thomas' brother Edmond died and then he inherited the manor. This was a saving grace for Thomas, for he was on the verge of going into debtor's prison. I did tell him to ask his brother before his death, but he said that he could not bother him at such a time. When Thomas settled in at the manor he took on the task of repairing and rebuilding parts that had begun to decay, bringing the house back to its former beauty. The bedchamber there was always mine and I had my own key. Thomas had décor and furnishings changed to my liking. It had an adjoining door to his and there was a four-poster bed and on it was a coverlet with embroidered peacocks and bed hangings to match. There was a large window which looked out onto the herb garden beneath and when I opened it of a morning its sweet scents would perfume the room. I had two chests for clothes and a table with a looking glass on it along with bottles and oils. A stand with pitcher and bowl stood in one corner and beside my bed was a table. On it was a candlestick or a lantern if I preferred. The floor in the room was scattered with lavender-scented rushes and the walls were dark oak panelled.

On a table of which I spoke about earlier I kept my gifts that had been given by those dear to me. One was a manicure set made of shell and a matching brush and comb. They had their own box, the lid was decorated with a carving of the sun and moon and a brass clasp. There was a further box, smaller, carved with leaves of myrtle in which I kept my trinkets such as rings, earrings and bracelets. It had a small brass key which was always kept upon my person.

In this room I found much peace of which I never derived anywhere in the house. In later years I would sit up in bed with my writing box, which Thomas had given me from Yule, upon my knees, writing down all my innermost thoughts. It was here I discovered my true spiritual self. Many a time I drifted into higher consciousness. There are hiding places in worlds far beyond this one, where I would reach out in my mind and draw upon the hidden power.

There was a ring given to me from Thomas, a silver ring with a salamander holding a Santa Cruz amethyst crystal, which I wore on the index finger of my right hand. On the small finger of my left hand I wore a garnet, a gift given to me also by Thomas. Another gift from Peter was a box containing a tarot deck that came from Venice, it was very pretty and hand painted.

Upon laying out the tarot deck I discovered to my amazement that it became second nature for me to be able to read from them with such clarity.

One early evening in late summer of 1591 I decided to dowse the grounds, for I had been told by Thomas of the Seven Crays – St Pauls Cray, St John's Cray; St Michael's Cray, Foots Cray, St Mary's Cray, North Cray and Crayford, all of which made up the seven-pointed star. There was a ley line (energy line) that ran straight through them and on the full moon, being at its height, I discovered that the power was immense. After discovering this happening I decided that I would speak of this to no one. I would wander off at first light and then before midnight when the moon was full I'd stand in its rays and soak in the energies from above and below.

Nearby in my secret space there was a fast running stream, so clear you could see the pebbles at the bottom. In the moonlight I would scry its waters whereupon visions would appear as clear as if it were flesh before my eyes. I remember once being shown a chalice, a book, a sword and triangle, then voices spake in my head, "This is truth. Look within oneself, into thine innermost soul and reach for what thou seekest. For what thou does see is nought but an enigma for thee to unfold." A further vision was that of a tarot card depicting The Fool, instantly changing into a Knight in silver armour. Suddenly I visualised Walter and heard the words, "beware! for he, thy lover, will betray thee".

He gave me patronage, advice and support as and when I needed it. He always said that my home will be forever open to you Christopher. My greatest regret however was bringing troubles into his house.

It became my sanctuary, somewhere I could escape to and be myself, where I was able to nurture the magical gifts that were within me.

Minstrel gallery at Scathebury Manor, Chislehurst, Kent (top)
Fireplace in Great Hall at Scathebury
Manor, Chislehurst, Kent (bottom)
(Photographs by Neville Harwood)

Chapter 11
The Rose

Phillip Henslowe, a local businessman, a man who could be a mean old fellow at times, owned the Rose playhouse but on the other hand he could be very generous, especially at feast days and holidays. He invested many monies into this new venture, at first it was rather plain, but due to building problems it had to be reconstructed in the early 1590s. The roof over the stage was made longer and the stage was altered so that more people could attend the plays. It was beautifully decorated with Tudor roses around the panels and around the pillars that could be removed. In the heavens (above the stage) were a throne, sun, moon and stars all brightly painted gold. Rush lights lit up the stage along with coloured lights hanging around for effect and at the side of the stage there were steps where the actors could make their entrance and exit.

The pit area was where the groundlings stood for half a penny, the seated areas around the sides of the stage, the lower galleries as they were called would cost you one penny and the upper galleries it would be two pennies, for this is where the nobility sat. In the pit floor area there were gutters for the rainwater to drain away. I would often sit on the edge of the stage.

The Rose had three entrances for the public at the front and they would be directed to different parts of the theatre. It had windows in the gallery area to let air in during the performances. The stage was made of polished wood that had a trap door cut into it. Sawdust and straw was strewn on the floor to keep the place clean after each evening's performance, which was often two or three. Henslowe would get everyone checking inside the theatre, in case of a fire. I remember, we had a fire one day, but fortunately it was quickly snuffed out. The Rose always kept barrels of water in the pit area, plus many buckets, for safety.

The costumes were made from the finest velvet, silk, linen and wool and trimmed with silver, gold and bright coloured lace. Some of the velvet and silk costumes were heavily embroidered in silver and gold. Phillip would boast that his costumes were the best of all the playhouses in London. The jewels to adorn the costumes would have fooled any thief, for they looked so real. Every play was full of magic and splendour. Henslowe's whores would make, clean and repair the costumes by day and sell their wares by the evening for their master at the playhouse.

At the back of the stage was the tiring rooms where the costumes and props were kept, plus a room where the actors could sleep between performances. A bookcase held all the manuscripts for the actors to read. Above the tiring rooms was a thunder-sheet for the special effects, pulleys for the backdrops and curtain scenery. Wires and harnesses were used to make an actor fly and ladders so that you could climb up to the roof area and balcony. Henslowe had an office at the back, which you had to go up a small flight of stairs, but he would not allow us to go there when he was counting his monies – much more monies that he would admit to. There was another room with plastered walls and fine ceiling from which you see the play.

My Truth

Outside of The Rose hazelnuts, roasted nuts, cakes, nosegays and other kinds of wares were sold. There were hostelries and a whore-house that was not far from Rose Alley. Sometimes the audience would jeer and shout, but they were told to keep quiet, but it all depends who you got in. The regulars seemed to be the best behaved. If you got a few on the later showings coming from the inns nearby who were drunk, they had to be thrown out, for there had been riots round these parts too.

Edward Alleyn, Ned as we called him, had a very powerful voice and we would oftimes hear it booming all around the theatre. When he took the leading role as Tamburlaine in one performance at The Rose, a lady in the audience who was with child was killed when a pistol that should have been loaded with blanks had been loaded with a live bullet. This caused great embarrassment for Phillip. The audiences would specially enjoy Tamburlaine and liked it very much when the King of Persia was bashing his brains out in a cage. They cheered when Tamburlaine was in his chariot, followed by two of his captives who were tethered to it. Audiences enjoyed the macabre acts; for we used pig's blood to make the actors look as if they were bleeding, the more the better. The boy actors were chosen for their beauty and they would use a pumice stone to rub their faces to remove any stubble and shave their legs. Often men in the audience would proposition the boys and wait for them after the theatre had closed. Ned would protect any boys who were being pestered in this way, as they were apprentice actors in his charge. I must confess there was an incident after one of my plays; Phillip and Ned caught a youth and me, whose name I do not wish to disclose, in an embrace. None of the other actors were present, as they had already left the theatre. After this I was told to leave.

The following day I was summoned to Ned and Phillip in their private room. The youth was there and we were both questioned. The youth insisted, backed up by me, that it was I complimenting him on his role in the play, afterwards he was allowed to leave. Ned then came over to me and put his arm about my shoulder, "Now Kit I knows thou hast a fancy for pretty boys, but both Phillip and I are responsible for them. This time there has been no complaint, so you were lucky it was us he saw and not the authorities, for there is enough said by the puritans, so no need to give them fuel for the fire Kit." I turned and faced Ned, "I promise you and Phillip it was nothing more than a kiss and embrace." Ned squeezed my shoulder before walking away. We consider the matter closed then said Phillip, "but remember, what you do behind closed chamber doors is your affair and what goes on here is ours, now you may leave."

Just as I was walking through the door both Phillip and Ned said, "where's that new play you promised?" I turned, smiled and said, "it will be in your hands Friday". As I was walking to the Anchor I thought to myself, I must take care, yes the play will be ready and I hope Phillip has the money. If he can get away with paying half to me he will, but if Ned is there I am sure I will get it in full. But if you owed money to Phillip or a play that was a different story he would expect it straight away. There was no peace with him, for many a time he would seek me out at the Anchor when I was eating. One time I got angry with him, "you never give me time to eat. Let me eat my victuals in peace man, you try the patience of a saint, leave me be, for you shall have your play when I am good and ready".

Chapter 12

Sir Roger Manwood

In my youth I was full of ambition and had a great passion for learning for this was recognised by my master at King's School. "We have here a promising young scholar." I once remembered him saying to a certain knight of the realm, when he visited the school on one occasion. This knight I speak of was Sir Roger Manwood, Chief Justice and Baron of the Exchequer, the most feared judge by many who came before him. He showed no mercy to those who were not truly repentant. His home was Hackington in Kent, a fellow countryman, and his motto was 'suffer children to come unto me'. Yes, he was a charitable man who gave help to the poor and patronage as well. He admired those who wished to better themselves, even though they may have come from a humble background. I became one of those who he gave patronage to. He showed much interest in my progress and he spoke with me at length on many subjects and to my father too. I guess he became very fond of me and as time went on, the fondness became that of a lover. At the age of thirteen I was raped and the man's name I offered to reveal, but I will speak of him later.

Sir Roger was kind to me and always encouraged me to go forward in the world. He told me that his wife adored him, but there was another part of him she could not fulfill. He gave me small gifts, paid all my fees and was much pleased when I passed my Scholarship. I was given a token by him and he said if ever I needed his help in any way, I was to send this token to him. He remained in my thoughts and I would meet up with him from time to time and when I was once before him in court, he was most lenient. At one time he was under investigation for accepting bribes, but in 1592 he became very ill and his mind was confused.

I wrote an epitaph for him and when writing this I remembered him as a man in his middle years, with greying hair down to his collar. A fresh ruddy complexion and short, neatly trimmed beard and moustache. Although he could hold a stern look in his dark eyes, there was something of a caring person there too. Broad in the chest and belly, which he remarked was due to fine living and then he would laugh. Behind closed doors he was a very different man to the judge on the bench. Upon visiting his home you could see he was a family man. His family were pleased to receive his epitaph from me. I remember, I found it hard not to shed a tear when I heard of his passing. I looked at a couple of the gifts he gave me and I couldn't stop reflecting back to those pleasant times of my youth.

Chapter 13
The School of Night

The school of night was first started in the 1580s by Sir Walter Raleigh and friends who were all of like minds. Men of learning and free thinking. There was Henry Percy, 9th Earl of Northumberland, well known to his friends as the Wizard Earl. A mathematician, Thomas Hariot, scientist Walter Warner, Carew Raleigh, Dr John Dee and many others.

Sir Walter and Henry, like myself and others wished to study the pathway of the soul, scientifically, spiritually and by metaphysics. The pathway of the soul, its journey in this life and of its existence in the after life. We looked at how the elements played their part in man's life and how the moon affected people's mind, such as people turning from sane to insane. How phases of the moon had magical power and forces that were stronger than you could ever imagine and be used for good or ill.

We did not believe that we were doing anything wrong, although we questioned the scriptures, we felt that man should question all things. Henry Percy was interested in astronomy and astrology, and the power of stones and gems. He had read from many ancient writings, how they were used to heal the sick and he discovered that they held much power.

We heard a lecture from Anthony Bacon on Plato's theories of Atlantis, this we found most intriguing. I did in particular and it prompted me to write a play which I called 'The Fall of Atlantis'. There was a lecture given by Dr John Dee on astrology. He explained how the planets affected people's lives and yes, he warned me that whatever happens is meant to happen, nothing you do could change it, as it is there at your birth. John White gave a lecture on the indigenous people of the Americas, explaining their strange customs, one of which was smoking the weed (tobacco) to help lift their spirits, and helping them to link with the gods.

We worked magical rituals and I along with Dr John Dee devised a 'tree of life' for our own purposes, to work with the Angel forces. These rituals helped us to take our minds higher, linking in to the Akashic Records and the Ascended Masters in the higher realms of light. On the tree were thirteen lights and thirteen angels. There was a seven pointed star painted on the floors of Scathebury, Mortlake and Durham House. The rooms were hidden from prying eyes and to my knowledge no-one ever discovered them.

The rituals were performed at the solstices and at certain phases of the moon. Candles were placed on the floor on each point and there were seven of us or sometimes thirteen, depending on the ritual we were to perform. According to our birth signs and the elements that represented them, we gave ourselves names – Bull Men; Salamander Men; Swan Men and Dragon Men.

Before we started each ritual, we washed in oils to cleanse our bodies (clean within and clean without), each member choosing their own oils which suited their body or needs. Then so that we were equal, we wore ceremonial gowns over our naked bodies. Worn around these gowns we had different coloured sashes with knots, some were tied and some weren't, depending on progression within the group. We greeted each

My Truth

other by touching one another's palms as this was from the Rosicrucian way, and we believed may have been done in the City of Atlantis. As I was the centre point, the hub of power, I had to be grounded within the mandala wheel which was devised by Dr John Dee and Henry Percy for our ceremonies. It was most important that throughout the ritual I was grounded in the energies and centred and balanced correctly. We would smoke the sacred pipe and tobacco that Walter Raleigh prepared for us, to take us to our higher self, as we passed it around the circle. We used runes and crystals, and a special sword as an athame (sacred sword or dagger). Walter called it the 'curved sword', it was only small and it had markings engraved on it, to do with the Qabala. It was not a sword for killing, only used for ceremonial purposes and believed to be connected with the Meonia, along with seven other swords.

Once we had formed a circle on the wheel, we then uttered words of the Qabala, each member saying the Qabalistic word associated with themselves. The Qabala was used to weave a spell, and to build up the energies like a serpent or spider. As with most things there is always a price, so if it all went wrong I had to pay the price, for I was the sacrifice. For you must sacrifice yourself to save those who are with you. John Dee was not happy with the way we mixed the energies and later withdrew from the group. I had knowledge from a good teacher whom I communicated with through my friend Robert Payne, so I reached a higher level of consciousness, a level that was far beyond comprehension. Robert always told me, "if you play with the Angels they will play with you".

We had to know the positions of the star and we would each move around the wheel in accordance with them. I had to move to each of the seven points of the star, one step wrong, would throw everything into disarray. The stepping was also in a sense, weaving and going forward. By doing this you can invoke thunder, lightning a tempest or other elements. We were told by Walter Raleigh that Indians of the Americas did this same type of ritual dance. We sometimes took ourselves to where we could see books and knowledge that had never been written, but were to be written. In many ways, we felt that the world was reverting back to a new beginning and we were playing our part in the Grand Design. Sometimes I became the star itself and laid within the centre. To us the star was the beginning and the end of all things. The beginning of the pathways, the joining and the end of pathways, all of which cross through the centre of the star. We believed that we could be re-born again and become another within the wheel. In the circle the members changed places, and in so doing we began to undestand that what was within in each of us. By being open with one another, in perfect love and perfect trust, our understanding and knowledge increased.

There were times when we would bring the positive and the negative together, the masculine and the feminine. Another member would join me in the centre of the circle, we would put our palms together, becoming 'one' with each other and once we touched it allowed the energies to flow between us. It seemed as if you were weightless, as if our bodies were one. I once said that in an act of making love, it is not just the physical, it is the spirits that have combined and takes one to one's higher self. As you can imagine there was a lot of energy built up during these ceremonies. Some of the members said they looked at me in the centre and I became light, with gold flashes of light from head to toe. This too was scientific, for we could prove that what shone from the physical was light, and that our spirits or even our physical being, can higher our vibrations, bringing about a change or metamorphosis.

I would wear a crown, a thin gold band that went across my forehead and around my head and sometimes had flowers in my hair. We used runes, each member having their own. I had a rune made from two triangles, forming a figure of eight or infinity. We also each had symbolic items such as sceptres and wands, which we used in our ceremonies.

We met at night because the elements are stronger and we were able to build up our energies much quicker. This is why the group was called the 'School of Night'. We experimented with a wide range of elements, including colour and crystals, like the Egyptians and Atlanteans would have done. The colours in the crystals gave off light and we felt that maybe these colours affected a person's subtle energy bodies or chakra energy centres.

We were experimenting with the light and how a person was attracted to a certain colour and if it had anything to do with their birth sign. I remember one time when we made a prism of light by cutting glass, which produced a rainbow shooting light through it. We then projected it forward to see what we were able to get from it. As an experiment we sensed a change in energies around us and felt tingling sensations up and down our spines.

In an experiment with me, I found I couldn't wear red, as it clashed with the colour of my hair, although I was able to wear deeper reds such as burgundy or maroon. If I wore a bright colour, or brighter colours, I started to feel anger inside me. Alright, I admit I did have a fiery temper, but certain colours made me feel uncomfortable. I used to like wearing black and my friends said this sometimes gave me an air of mystery. There were times I used to like wearing greens and browns, as to me these was earthy and restful colours, which I felt comfortable with.

By experimenting with gemstones we discovered that we were attracted to certain ones. The stone I was attracted to mostly was the amethyst, I couldn't get on with diamonds. Walter Raleigh was very fond of pearls. The two main stones we worked with was green and red. The red, the most powerful, was a ruby, which had a blue cast when held up to the light. The green stone restrained you.

A magician always wears stones in his rings, not for wealth I may had, but for power and the energy that comes from the stones. We had a staff with a crystal ball at its centre representing the world and twisted around it were two silver serpents. Whenever we experimented with the elements we always wore silver, for we believed that the energies of silver reacted with the elements in a different way to gold. But in the circle the water signs wore silver and the sun signs wore gold. How you position yourself in relation to the compass points can make a difference. I found by positioning myself facing north, I was able to write better and if I needed inspiration I faced the east. We found that energies affected man particularly ley lines (energy lines that run underneath the earth). In Pagan times man used these energy lines like a map to move around the country. Often these energies ran underneath the ground of churches and temples at pre-Christian sites. It is said that one such line runs through Glastonbury. The symbol of the dragon is an indication of such sites, this is why you see the dragon on many of the churches and temples.

Owing to some of the members in the group becoming egotistical and wanting to use the energies for selfish greed and power, we disbanded. The group was made up of an inner and outer group, and it was the outer group who were the egotists. The inner group were the one's who wanted to work on a spiritual level, working with the Qabala, elements and Angel forces. In the circle I was known as the Morning Star, in Roman, it was Venus and Aphrodite in Greek. In orthodox belief it was Lucifer or the devil to some. In fact, it represents love and light and is on the Tree of Life.

I drew diagrams and the rituals, but the formula and patterns I kept in my head. Thomas Walsingham had his suspicions about what was going on, so he told me to leave the meetings, as he sensed there was danger. It wasn't long after this the whole group disbanded, for the Church was getting suspicious of our activities.

Some years after this I met a priest I was working with, who had done much research in the Church of Rome. He told me much about the hidden writings and texts in the vaults and that he had access. He once took me and showed me many of these writings, of which I found contained ancient knowledge that was no stranger to me.

Mandala Wheel as used by the School of Night
and devised by Christopher Marlowe.
(Illustration by Neville Harwood

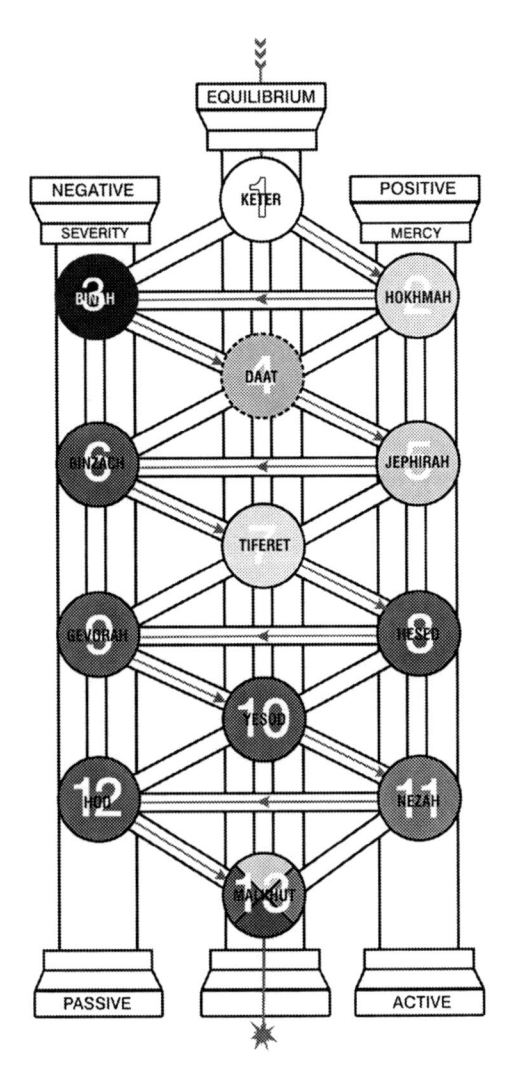

Qabala Tree devised by Christopher
Marlowe and Dr John Dee.
(Illustration by Neville Harwood)

Chapter 14

My visits to Scotland with Sweet Robin

Lord Burleigh was keeping connections with Scotland close to his chest, there were visits that were even kept from her Majesty, for there was a need to have an ear at the court of King James, as they were still in the old faith and who were plotting with Spain. There were those Catholics who were living in hope that when the heretic Elizabeth dies the new king will give sympathy to their cause. So it was as well to have a listening ear, for the court of King James was so magnificent as that of our own English court, but nonetheless it was friendly and we behaved in a goodly manner. When first I encountered the king of Scots, I tried to see his mother's books, for she was such a beauty and yet he was bodily disfigured and short of stature. But I could see through that physical outlook and inside was a strange character with an astute mind, no fool was he, but this I had seen in Robert Cecil, or Pygmy was what the Queen would call him. Although the king was married he had the same persuasion as myself, for he would embrace and kiss those young pretty men, even at court. The king spoke with me and said that he had heard of my success and he suggested I write a Scottish play for him. Robin said that he would be king one day and I replied, "yes", but the Catholics need not put their hopes upon him and if there were those plotting against the queen, he would have no part, lest it hindered his path to the English throne. I had to observe and listen, for there had been mention of Arabella Stuart settling upon the English throne and another candidate was Ferdinando Lord Strange. The Holy Church of Rome was hell-bent on regaining control of the English throne at whatever cost to life and limb.

Before the troubles came I was in privy with Lord Burleigh and he told me that he had mooted to the king of the Scots that I would make a good tutor for his young prince and of course be a permanent spy, as I was to keep a watchful eye on the comings and goings. There were others he had in mind, but I was the best and King James was interested in me, for he asked me questions about my persuasion. But this conversation he said had to go no further and I should await instruction.

Robert was unaware of what could have transpired, but what I was sure of, he would always reap his rewards. The main plot was that regarding Lord Strange. I myself found him not the kind of man seeking to take the throne and from my dealings, found nothing when speaking to Thomas Kydd, who often did secretarial work for him. He was also working in his noverint trade copying documents and with a little coaxing he was able to tell me of what was in their contents and what he told me was that Lord Strange wanted none of it.

Chapter 15

Coining in Flushing

There was another plot hatching against our queen. Robert Poley who was now in full control of those agents in the Low Countries had received intelligence from Michael Moody, who had gained the confidence of the conspirators in Brussels. I recall that it was early on in 1592 when I was granted papers to travel to Flushing in Holland. There I was to meet up with Richard Baines and Gilbert Gifford, a goldsmith from London. We had to seek out and report on those coining, so Gilbert would encourage those Catholics who were desperate for monies as they had forfeited all when they left England. Gilbert knew that they needed monies to service and finance their cause.

Lord Burleigh had knowledge of Sir William Stanley and others seeking out coins to finance their campaigns and plots to put another Catholic monarch on the English throne, with the blessing of Spain and the Holy Church of Rome.

Gilbert was a fine craftsman and his English coins were the best forgeries by far, but his Dutch and Spanish he needed to perfect. Richard marvelled at this and asked me if I would secretly give him some of the coining. I asked him for what purpose did you need these coins, but he would give me no explanation. Myself I had fully trusted Richard, for although he always stood by the fact he had recanted his Catholic faith, in me there was always a doubt of him in double-dealing. He knew why we were here and that my purpose was to encourage Catholics to come out, by purporting to be one myself.

In Flushing I was instructed to seek out those publishers and printers who were smuggling libellous pamphlets and books to those catholic plotters in England. I found a man I could trust and he also promised to print and publish my works that I was unable to release in England openly, but could be smuggled in and it was he who helped me when I came to England for a short while, during my exile.

All the time I was there I had the feeling that Richard Baines was scheming and did not want me there. And my gut feeling proved me right, yet again.

Everything was going well until on the evening upon my return I found that I was under arrest, along with the goldsmith, but not Richard. He admitted he was the informer and it was I not he who was turning to the Catholic faith, this I denied. The Governor Sir Robert Sidney questioned each of us in turn, after listening to me he told me that it was not for him to decide, but Lord Burleigh. So not to be discovered as agents, Gifford and I had to return under Lloyd's escort. It was a very serious matter and a hanging one, for it was treasonable.

When we arrived back in England Burleigh and Henage questioned us all. I explained myself and gave the information, which I had gathered. I was told that Baines had got in before me and that I should have reported the matter first, for it was a foolish mistake on my part that I accepted this. It wasn't that he did or did not believe me, but Henage said that if Baines were given any more work, he would be left to his own devices, but watched from a distance. The goldsmith was imprisoned with me for what should have been three months, but I was released after one week to go on other business and the goldsmith methinks not long after. Once released, I was able to gather up information.

This information I passed on to Lord Burleigh and there was also a pamphlet I tracked down that alluded to an uprising financed by Spain. It was a plot to place an English nobleman on the throne, who will be in time persuaded to take up the crown on the assassination of our Queen and her Council.

There was to be more to this episode than met the eye, but it was ongoing and still being investigated after my exile. Suffice it to say, I shall reveal more on this in my next book.

Chapter 16
The Last Act

It is January in the year of Our Lord 1593. As Thomas embraced me, wishing me health, wealth and prosperity for the New Year ahead, I felt a deep foreboding within my breast. Standing back from me, hands resting upon my shoulders, a questioning look in his eyes, he spoke, "Kit, what ails thee?" Placing my arms around his waist and pulling him towards me, holding him tight, ah … 'tis nothing," I said, "nothing to worry thee."

We broke our fast and Thomas spoke of his plans to marry one beautiful and bright Audrey, "but there will always be a place in my heart for you Christopher" and he leaned forward and put his hand in mine, and "in your bed of course". I replied, "what about her, for it would hurt her would it not?" He said, "what she doesn't know about, won't hurt her", wiping his mouth with his napkin. "Well Christopher I have business to attend to, letters and bills, all boring stuff, but important. So you have all the morning to yourself." He then got up and left the room. I pondered for a moment then a quiet voice broken the peace, "have you finished good sir". I looked up and there before me stood a young serving girl, neatly dressed in a brown woollen dress and wearing a white apron and bonnet. Her face was shiny and her cheeks rosy, so when she smiled back at me, some of the foreboding left my mind. "Yes, you may take it away." I then got up from the table and went upstairs to my bedchamber and laid there for a while pondering over in my mind what shall I do next, for there is so much I want to write and yet I am tied up in my mind.

Then later that morning, walking in the woods that I so loved, the air cool and crisp, I looked around me and felt a sense of sadness that maybe I would only visit here a few more times. There was a silence. I felt that this year would be one full of uncertainties. I could not explain to myself why this deep melancholy had descended upon me.

Returning to the manor I joined Thomas for a mid-day meal. He was full of high spirits and talked with me of his plans to restore the manor. Work was to commence in the spring and he was confident that the proposed renovations would return the manor to its original state, it having been much neglected when inherited previously by his elder brother, Edmund. Before I could stop myself I turned to him saying, "It does not matter, Thomas, for I will not be here to see it."

Thomas's expression changed suddenly to one of concern. "Christopher, what sayest thou? Art though ailing? I wish not to lose thee. We must make haste to a physician." Clasping his arm I spoke with a confidence I did not feel. "No, I am well, Thomas. Maybe it is the unknown that concerns me."

Having filled my tankard with ale Thomas handed it to me saying, "Come Christopher, drink this, it will makest thee feel much better." Finishing my drink and placing the tankard upon the table I bid to take my leave. I felt weary and the need to retire. I climbed the winding staircase to my chamber, whereupon I lay down deep in thought. Beyond explanation I felt that I wanted to weep. The tears ... the tears flowed uncontrollably. I turned over to bury my face in the pillow so as not to disturb my friend. In my sorrow I finally slept.

My Truth

I awoke to Thomas's enquiring voice. "Christopher, shallst thou take repast today? Wouldst thou prefer supper in thy chamber?" He sat at my bedside, a look of concern upon his face. "Why weepest thou? What ails thee?"

I tried to reassure him. "Worry not, Thomas. As I spoke of before, 'tis just the uncertainty."

With serious expression Thomas replied. "Christopher, thou must start to change the company thou dost keep. It is known that thou still visits Walter and follows his damned views. You must take care and watch your table talk."

"Do not trouble thyself, Thomas, 'tis only occasionally I visit with him. My playmaking is more important, for it is where my heart lies."

At this point Thomas turned to me and said, "There are times, Christopher, I worry that thou mix betwixt playmaking and reality. These men that thou associate with are dangerous and exist only for their own ends. They care nothing for you." "Sweet Robin has more care for you than he, and has a heart made of ice, I am sure." I answered quickly in defence of Walter, "Walter loves me. I know that to be true."

But Thomas would not hear of this. "Christopher, the only person for whom Walter bears love is himself. He is not all that he seems. I know that thou lies with him and I have accepted it, but hoped that it would be only for a short while."

"Yes, I do keep peace with him, for he is high in the queen's favour, despite his troubles in the past where he fell from grace."

"But Christopher, if thoust have knowledge of any treason against Our Sovereign Lady thou must tell me. Thou owest me that at least."

"Thomas, thou knowst that I will always love you despite what has gone before. And I will never betray thee. If any danger were to befall thee I would protect thy name to the death." Upon saying this I took his hand and pulled him to me, feeling his manner to be cold. The touch of his hand was a chill within my own. I needed him so much. It had been a long time since he had lain with me. I felt I must speak. "Come lie with me, Thomas."

But he pulled his hand away. "I cannot, Christopher," and so saying left the room.

I sat there alone with my thoughts 'til dusk fell and a knock came upon the door. I bid them enter. It was young Alex with a tray of food for me. Placing it upon the table he lit a taper from the glowing embers of the neglected fire and proceeded to light the candles. "You need some light, sir." Rekindling the fire and placing logs upon its now blazing core he promised to return with a fresh supply of logs when I had finished my repast. He asked if I had need of anything, but I replied that I had not and thanked him. After he had left my bedchamber I picked at my meal, my appetite not too good, yet as always I enjoyed the custard tart, it was the best I have ever tasted.

Alex duly returned to remove my tray, dutifully bringing more fuel for the fire. I requested a pitcher of water and upon its arrival poured it into the bowl, washing myself and preparing for bed. I lay down upon my four-poster bed, the curtains partially drawn around me, the moonlight shining in through the window. In my half wakefulness I did not hear Thomas enter, but was suddenly aware of him as he stood beside me in the moonlight. He came to me and we embraced. I felt the warmth of him again, and that night we were together. The passion was fulfilled.

But as Thomas slept beside me, my heart questioned whether he had come to me out of love or pity. I felt very much that people never really understood my frustrations. When I think of these people who scorned me for my manner, they had not half my wit.

Thinking back to that time in 1593 when I was at Scathebury with Thomas, I recall that he left my bed before dawn. I had lain in the same spot where he had lain so that I could feel him still. It was as if he were there with me. There was a bond between us that no-one could break. We were bonded as souls. With Thomas I always felt protected and safe. As I lay there in the dawn light I felt as if he had only come to me in pity, my feelings were mixed. I never mentioned it to him for I did not want to offend him or spoil what was important to me. The lovemaking as well as the spiritual was important to me. I had a great appetite for lovemaking. Thomas always said to me that one man was never enough for me and really he was right. I would have settled with one had things not changed.

There was also another man that I came to love, William Shakespeare. I educated him in the art of blank verse. He was a gentle sort, with a good sense of humour, willing to learn. I saw within him the gift of writing and with a little tutoring from me I knew that I would make a playmaker of him yet. He shared my lodgings and we were firm friends.

But my mind wanders ... I left my bed and opened the window. I felt the chill of frosty air. I looked across the fields and felt to myself that I must write another poem. I had not yet decided who I was going to write about, but Thomas would be there somewhere. I stood there daydreaming, thinking of where this year was going to take me. I felt that there was going to be much unrest in the city, and at court. There were those who were on the side of Lord Deveraux, Earl of Essex; and those who favoured Sir Walter Raleigh; both favourites of the queen. I had been, and am still now, searching for information upon Sir Walter's dealings. I have not yet told Thomas of what I have discovered about Sir Walter. I know that they are on friendly

Brenda Harwood

terms for they both disagree with the government's policies. Methinks that I have got in too deep and that my heart is torn in many ways. I will always be loyal to Thomas, but Walter I am not sure of. Thomas is friendly towards him, but on the other hand I can see he does not trust him.

Walter is a man who is much like me in many ways. He has a fiery passion. There is a love or hate relationship between us and I am torn between two fires. If it came that I had to inform to Cecil upon Walter's dealings I do not wish to incriminate Thomas. This is where I feel so torn. Walter is a very powerful man, the richest man in all England. I know of his dealings with Spain, even though he says he hates them. He has smuggled gold bullion and jewels behind the Queen's back. She knows nothing of its existence. Nay, she does not. He has it hidden everywhere. He has a man who is a gold dealer and he takes the jewels to sell for Sir Walter. A certain amount of money is given to the queen, but not all the spoils. His sailors were loyal to him, and they would do the smuggling to whatever destination they are instructed.

What angered him at the time of the Spanish Armada and the English victory, was that sailors came back from fighting for England, many of them wounded, their families starving, and the queen refused to pay their wages. Walter Raleigh was angry, those men had fought for queen and country and she refused to think about paying them a penny. And she was celebrating the victory with no thought for expense. After that Walter decided not to give the queen everything. He gave the sailors some of the spoils as recompense. Walter was also displeased with the government, he believed men should have freedom of speech. He was not pleased with Her Majesty for not paying Sir Francis Walsingham for his work in the Low Countries, for the man died penniless. Walsingham had to put all his personal monies into funding the spy network and the queen owed him thousands of pounds, yet he died without receiving a penny of it and his widow was left with scarcely anything. Thomas, as a Walsingham, had hoped to take over the running of the spy network, but Henage and Robert Cecil must have been promised the position long before Francis died.

There has been talk that Sir Walter is in league with Spain and could be helping the Stanley's, for his own ends of course. He also mentioned to me that he was going on an expedition to find the Lost City of Gold and its buried treasure. It is but a legend I've been told, but Walter has spoken to those who had knowledge of it. What I was to discover is whether he was going to use this treasure to finance the Stanley's plot. I heard it from Sweet Robin that the King of Scots dislikes Sir Walter, so I fear when the Queen dies, 'tis best he leaves this land.

Upon one of our meetings I was scrying a crystal ball and in it I saw the 'block and axe', in shock I dropped the ball and it shattered. I warned Walter to be wary of those around him who wish to see his head on a spike, but he would have none of it. He laughed, but I knew all was not well for him and the matter was never mentioned again.

I decided that once this matter was finished, I would speak to Thomas asking him if I may retire from the service. I could then continue with translations, my plays and poetry, for that is where my heart lies, not in a world of lies, death and deceit.

After my sojourn at Scathebury I then returned to London and the theatre, for there was new plays to be written, hoping that there would be changes for the better. No more demands put upon me from the secret work, but this was not to be, for it was not long before I received a letter from Sweet Robin. He had been away and his master Lord Burleigh needed him again to travel to James of Scotland with important letters from her majesty. The Catholics in England were hoping that if he became king, he would give them the freedom to worship. And there were also those secret catholics here and in Scotland who were plotting with Spain to put a Catholic monarch back on the English throne and dispatch the heretic bitch, Elizabeth.

So we set out for Scotland in early spring, there was an icy wind blowing and it grew even colder before we found an inn. Robert told me that last time he went the king was impressed with me and that I should write a Scottish play. "Well Kit, if you wish to make favour that would be a good play to write next, maybe performed at the Scottish court." I thought to myself that would be, but which king? We arrived at Court and Robin gave me an instruction to pick up a letter elsewhere, but I am not at liberty to tell.

Upon talking to Robin he said, "there was talk abroad to put either Arabella Stuart on the throne or young Ferdinando Lord Strange or maybe one of the Percy's". He then looked straight at me, "have you anything to tell me, for you are well in favour with those men". "I have heard nothing as yet." "But I am sure Christopher you would tell me," and then we carried on our journey home.

I met with Robin once more before he left again for the Low Countries. "You worked with Thomas Kydd did you?" "Yes, he wrote for Lord Strange". He also did some private work as his old trade of noverint, copying documents for him." Robin sat back in his chair, "that's interesting, did you see what was in them?"

"No, but with a little coaxing, he was able to tell me the contents, but nothing that would interest us." "Remember Christopher what I told you, if you happen to visit him again keep a look out through his papers." I told Robin that I had left some papers there, so that would give me a good reason to pay him a visit. Tapping my arm, "well Christopher keep it to yourself, I shall be seeing you on my return, and try to keep out of trouble."

My Truth

There was unrest in the City, the apprentices had started to vent their anger over the immigrants taking their jobs and there were placards and threats of violence. I felt uncomfortable about this, so I went to the country, but as I said earlier, I had a foreboding feeling all was not well.

Upon my arrest those in the Privy Council such as Robert Cecil questioned me. I was shown a paper and note. The paper was one of which Thomas Kydd said belonged to myself, a heretical document questioning the deity of Christ. I explained that Thomas was an innocent man as he insisted and that he had copied it for me. It was well- known that I was once a student of divinity and I had interests in many such theories. And I tell thee, there was a copy of such a document at King's School. I was reminded that Thomas Kydd had worked for Lord Strange, "yes like myself a playmaker". We are not talking of playmaking, but plots by his master and furthermore your blasphemy, sedition and not forgetting other counts we are looking into. "What do you mean sedition?" Then I was shown a notice, which was taken off a church door, it was signed Tamburlaine, inciting hatred towards the immigrants. "But I know nothing about or had any part in this, I swear, please believe me." "Your blasphemous talk abroad, like the jibe you made against the sour-faced puritans. You have been warned before." Yes, I confess when in my cups I have been known to, but meant no great harm. There are those who have taken great offence. I was then alone with Robert Cecil. "My father must follow this through, we know you have done us good service and you must think hard upon while you are on bail, where your loyalty lies. If there is information you can tell us, then maybe we could spare your life, keep you for evidence and I do believe you that you didn't write the papers, it was not your style."

My thoughts on the way back to my lodgings went back to Thomas Kydd. I decided to visit him. He lay there on stinking straw, his hands and body broken, they had tortured him. He could hardly recognise me through his pain. "Why did you let them do this to me?" "I didn't, you should have rid yourself of those papers." Don't you mean, rid myself of you, Judas." "I never betrayed thee, please believe me". He then turned away from me, weeping like a child. I gave the gaoler some monies. "Please make sure his wounds are tended and some extra food is given to him. That night I slept but one hour of sleep. My thoughts were, "who hath done this to me, who signed that Tamburlaine, for who hath done this deed upon me?"

I was not permitted back to Scathebury, as Thomas Walsingham would not allow me to go, only upon his request, because I was under investigation. At 10 of the clock every day I had to report to the Star Chamber and I was not permitted to leave England. So I stayed in my lodgings in London. I spent my time writing and ate at inns, but my appetite hardly existed. I just had to wait until I was instructed on what to do by Thomas. Thomas was to await the decision about my future. He had friends in the Star Chamber and sent word to Robert Poley, asking if he could return home earlier than expected. Both Thomas and Walter were afraid of what I would say under torture. I also had in my possession minutes of meetings of the School of Night. No one else knew of them. They were in my lodgings, but I had hidden them carefully and eventually took them away with me when I left England. Robin asked me for them when he saw me, but they were mine. There were no names mentioned, for they contained simply theories and discussions. The Star Chamber wanted evidence of what had been going on in the School of Night, anything that was unorthodox was punishable by death or imprisonment. The papers would have been found offensive to the Church and State. I took them to Padua and kept them close. I finally left them with Peter. It was a very difficult time between 19th and 30th May for me. I had a letter from Thomas to visit Scathebury and fetch Will Shakespeare with me. Myself, Will and Thomas had a meeting at Scathebury. It was Thomas's decision and I was invited to visit for the meeting and stay the night. But he said he wanted the advice of Robin as well and as to whether he would be willing to take me as an agent on the Continent. I said what about the plays and it was Will who offered to put his name to them. He made that decision because we were very close friends and he felt that he didn't want my work to go unseen, so I had no choice, but I won't say that I was happy. It was either that or my plays would never be seen at all. Although it was to be another name for the writer of my plays, Will said what he did was for the love of his friend. Thomas agreed, with the proviso that when he died the truth would be stated in his will so that Will would not have it on his conscience. Will accepted that and said that he was happy to visit me to discuss the plays, and in secret I would stay at Scathebury or at an inn in St Albans or Dunstable. Eventually there would be an arrangement for Robin or another to collect and bring the papers between them. If there was a chance for me to come back to England we couldn't meet anywhere near the city, so we chose the inn in St Albans, the White Hart, because it was on Watling Street, a main travelled road. We did also choose to meet in Dunstable, methinks at the Cross Keys. There was another one in the town centre that was called, strangely enough, the White Hart. I could stay also at the apothecary's. All of this was done in shrouded secrecy.

I bear no malice against Will for we were bonded souls and minds, we could work together. Although we were apart I could send a thought and strangely enough he could write it. Will did not write so many of the plays that are named as his, but he had many excellent ideas, and good plots. He was good with comedy, whereas I myself was not very good on humour. My sense of humour was maybe not so developed. I would not say it was dull, but I was not so well on the bawdy humour. But Will was a natural with the comedy. He enjoyed a joke – a jest.

I wish those who read my book not to scorn Will for he was only doing what he was asked of and he like myself carried the burden upon his shoulders. He kept my secret well and we remained firm friends up to his untimely death, which I don't believe was of natural causes. He wrote me of his fears, but alas there was nought I could do to save my friend. But I thank him for his love and friendship and the years he gave me when I was in exile. I would weep when I think upon the burden I put upon him, for the truth lies in my verse.

To save those who were dear to me, I decided to give Cecil what he wanted, and in return my freedom not in this country, but resign myself to become an agent on the Continent and the Low Countries. I had to discuss this with Sweet Robin on his return, but Thomas informed me that he would be instructed. When Robin returned after his visit with Thomas, he visited me at my lodgings. It was late evening and I was writing. I had mixed feelings, was he to be "my saviour or my executioner", I thought. "Well Christopher you have really done it this time." "I promise you Robin, I have been duped." "Well, what have I told you, take care never to get in too deep. I shall do my best to discover who, but for now, 'tis your neck we have to save. To give us time to think, you keep your mouth shut and do as you are told until you see me at Eleanor Bull's on 29 May. All is arranged one way or another, so leave everything to Thomas and me. Oh, and by the way, Thomas Kydd will be released soon I believe. Thomas Walsingham will be visiting you after dark on the morrow." He put his hand on my shoulder. "Don't worry, I will do my best." He then left; I opened a bottle of wine and drank myself to sleep.

The following evening I lay on my bed waiting for Thomas to call. Many thoughts were on my mind and what I must do before whatever becomes of me. As I came to the end of my thoughts, there was a knock at the door. I opened it and there stood Thomas, I have to admit the only man I really ever loved and I had brought shame on him. I don't know what come

My Truth

over me, but I just wept uncontrollably. He came in and closed the door behind him and held me in his arms. I couldn't stop weeping. "Christopher, what is done is done, I had warned you in the past about careless table talk and I regret ever involving you with Sir Walter Raleigh, for he has not helped, but mark my words, he shall pay one day. I know you've been foolish, but on the other hand you have a fine mind and that we must protect at all costs, but everything has its price and so does your freedom. Exile is a painful word, but 'tis better than the rope or the stake, for I couldn't bear to watch that." He then released me from his arms and I dried my tears. Thomas poured us both a goblet of wine. We both sat down. "You've been so good to me in many ways and look how I have repaid you, all I have ever done is let you down. I always lose those I love and hurt them.

"Marry Audrey and forget me, you deserve much better. I am just no good to either you or myself. After this ask no more of you or your lady." "Christopher, we all make mistakes and we have to learn, but on the other hand I know it was not you who wrote those libellous pamphlets in the churchyard. It is not your style and I know you sometimes say what you don't really mean. But you left yourself wide open and there are those who will twist your words to suit themselves. As for you being no good, that simply isn't true and you know it. Before I was lord of the manor you was there for me and gave me your love and friendship, which meant more to me than anything. Although you will be beyond the sea, not even that will keep us apart and I know we have not been as close for a while, but that don't mean that I don't love you. What has happened has made me realise what I am losing, but we can make the most of the time we have. So let's not talk of leaving for the now and just make the night last and ask the gods to hold back the break of day a little longer." He then put down his drink, took my hand and we retired to my bedchamber. It was like the first time we had made love, I had never been loved with such meaningful worth and passion, for nothing mattered or time did stand still. The gentleness of his touch and his kisses helped me to forget for a while and reassured me that he still loved me. Between our lovemaking my thoughts went back to the poem I was writing for him at Scathebury, 'Hero and Leander'. I stretched out my hand, "so was his neck in touching, the white of Pelope's shoulder. I could tell ye, how smooth his breast was and how white is belly, and with a smile I thought and whose immortal fingers did imprint that heavenly path with many a curious dint, that runs along his back." "Christopher if you should die before I, your heart shall be brought back and buried at Scathebury." "Thomas, let us not speak on death, for there is no death, for the soul lives on" and with those words I kissed and lay in his arms. When I awoke he had gone, leaving the imprint on the pillow where he laid. I lay there for a moment, for I could feel him still and smell the scent of his body. When I awoke again on the table beside the bed was a green leather pouch and in it was a gold chain with a small seven-pointed star and a note scribbled by Thomas. "I believe to be the star of protection, keep it always. Wear it with my love and friendship, I shall try and see you before you leave."

The time for the meeting was drawing ever closer and I needed to clear a few things up, but on the other hand not make people suspicious. My lodgings were well paid in advance, as when I had money I always made sure I had a place to sleep and write. Food was not a problem, since my landlady was a kindly old woman and would always bring me a bowl of her stew or loaf of bread and cheese. My rooms were always cleaned and linen washed. I cleared up all papers that were not important and burned them. I packed a couple of books, some papers and clean linen, for tomorrow I was to meet my fate at Eleanor Bull's.

While I lay here unable to sleep, thoughts drifted back to those gone before, Tom Watson, Robert Greene, who gave me a warning before he left this world. There were times when you never knew whether he was your friend or enemy, you are both well out of it. When I saw Thomas Nashe he asked me how I was and that he was hoping to start a new poem, which was difficult at times as he had been ill for a short while. But now all was looking better and that we must meet. I said "yes, it would be good", but in my heart I knew that we would never see each other again, not in this life.

Christopher Marlowe
in his late twenties
by psychic artist
David Calvert-Orange

Chapter 17

Deptford

It was about mid morning, 29 May when I finally arrived at Dame Eleanor Bull's lodging house. The day was not too hot, with a clear blue sky and sunshine. I found Robert sitting in the garden drinking his ale, he bade me join him, then asked me what I would like, "the same as yourself", I replied. Then he leaned forward towards me and whispered, "I have reserved rooms upstairs, so when we have supped we can retire for a while, then we can have a talk." "Don't look so glum man at least you haven't finished up like Penry." I replied, "he's the least of my problems, soon he will be well out of it, but mine have just begun".

Whilst we were sitting there Dame Eleanor came over to us. We both greeted her. She was wearing a grey satin dress with silver lace trim on the bodice. A fine looking woman for her years, plump but shapely with well rounded breasts. She smiled and her eyes sparkled, "I trust you young gentlemen will find all to your liking and Kit Marlowe when will you have that poem you keep promising me." At this point she was called upon and left us. She kept a fine house, good food, the best in these parts and a clean and comfortable bed. She only accepted gentlemen and ladies and it was a safe house for agents on government business. Just before we were going, Mistress Bull arrived holding a letter, which she gave to Robin. We then went inside to our bedchamber and Robin instructed her that we did not wish to be disturbed, only if it is urgent.

We entered our bedchamber, the door was closed and all was silent. Robin gestured that I take a seat, this was one of the best beds, a four-poster bed with red curtains and coverlet, a wooden chest at the foot, a table for one to eat a meal and two chairs by the fire. The panelling was made of oak. "This is our chamber, and there is another next door," Robin said. He then sat down on one of the chairs and opened the seal on his letter. By now I was feeling quite nervous and Robin noticed this. "Relax man for heaven's sake, while I read this letter." So I tried to do what I was bid, there was a long silence then Robin looked at me and pointed to the bottle of wine and two goblets on the table. "Pour us each a drink Christopher." I did what he suggested and then sat down.

Should have been more careful who you spoke to, for Baines has put together a list of all your blasphemous talk and so on. I warned you to take care and never tell where you are about. Your chances Christopher of going to Scotland at this moment are not looking good. You will have to take care of whom you trust in future, for you trust too easily. You must learn to see both sides, you may have seen Cholmeley as another free-thinker but he his not be trusted. So this is something you will have to learn. "Robert Cecil needs you, for in the past, yes you have served us well." "But he seemed trustworthy." "Christopher, nobody is trustworthy in the world of espionage."

"I have been informed by Robert Cecil that in the future you may be used at the Court of King James for the Spanish are waiting to land there, but when we don't know." He then took a sip of his wine. "You now work for me of course, as I am still under the instruction of the Cecil's but from this day on you are instructed by me." "So where do I go from here?" "Well, before we discuss that we had better eat." I didn't really feel like food but to please my host I ate a little and when the meal was over Robin then revealed to me what he wanted me to know. I should leave on the morrow and could hide at Scathebury, as Thomas knew a safe hiding place there. I was to wait for his instruction before taking ship at nightfall for the Low Countries. Papers and a new identity would be arranged and I could pose as a Catholic priest. "You've done it before and carried it off well, Chrstopher. You can carry on writing and give the papers to me, for I shall bring them back to England, or we can arrange for you in time, to come back, in secret of course. But you must do and go where I send you, that way you will remain safe. I know all the safe houses and lodging houses in France, Low Coutries, Spain, Venice and Padua. But I hope this has made you realise you must not trust anyone but me."

Although Robin was a well-known rogue, he was the best man the Cecil's ever had. I had no choice but to trust him. Robin gave me advice on how to survive on the Continent and then after supper we talked. "I remember we once talked of the Meonia stone that once belonged to Mary Queen of Scots, but it was never found amongst her belongings. It is said there were several artefacts that belonged to Mary, a stone known as the 'eye of fire', one other set into a silver scarab beetle and curved sword that allegedly belonged to Akhenaten, all of this came about at the time of the Babington Plot. Yes, I do remember having a lecture on Hermetic teachings. Robin then gave me a sharp look. "Was this at one of Raleigh's meetings?" I kept silent, then replied, "yes". "Did Anthony give you anything for me or any item for safe keeping?" Knowing that I still had in my care these artefacts except the Meonia stone, in my own mind wished to keep them for security. "No Robin, he gave me nothing." Robin looked at me suspiciously and said "we will leave it for now".

We spent the rest of the evening talking and what he had planned for the morrow. We then retired to bed and we took comfort in each other. When the morrow came Nick Skeres and Ingram Frizer arrived. Nick was always eager to serve, he helped in the Babington Plot and Robin paid him well. He would sell is own soul for a price. Ingram worked for Thomas Walsingham in the running of the estate at Scathebury, and I know he was a cony-catcher in his time and that's why he calls for a favour now and again. Ingram had a wife and two daughters and a son who died as an infant, from what Thomas told me. Something Ingram did not want to discuss, for it was too painful a memory for him. When he arrived he gave me a letter sent from Thomas. It had details of where I was to hide on the estate and I was to keep well out of sight until instructed where to go to next. Robin had it all planned. All of us had a few drinks and a meal in the garden, then I went up to Robin's chamber, he followed leaving the others behind. He closed the door. "Well Christopher collect your belongings, it is time to take your leave until we meet in a few days time. There is a horse saddled up in the stable, it's the chestnut mare in the corner of the stable. She will carry you safely. Now be on your way." We then kissed and embraced. "Let this be a lesson to you Christopher, at least you have your life." I then followed him down the back stairs and out to the stable to collect the horse. I took her out of the stable, climbed into the saddle and rode quietly out of the yard. I was made to travel forth without my cloak, to let base clouds o'er take me in my way, hiding thy bravery in their rotten smoke.

My story continues in the next book 'I Live Again'.

Far memory by Kit
3rd March 1998

When at last I resigned myself to a spirit existence, no longer of the flesh. My mind then was set upon reflecting back on my full life. Remembering my writing which I had left behind me at my passing, and before the fever took my mind. There was much I wrote regarding those I had known, loved, and hated, for there was bitterness within my heart mingled with self-pity. For my mind was set that it was the fault of all but me, but I had no one to heal me, until I entered the spirit realms. It was there when healed, though not completely, I was able to see clearer through the cloud of hurt. I spent many hours, I say hours but time hath no meaning in the unseen world, upon meditation and looking back at what I had done. Some I could not face, this I was told was 'facing my conscience' and this I had to do before I could progress. There was no hell that I was told of, but tolerance and guidance coupled with love that you would have for a misguided child. I was wrapped in a blanket of blue light, helping to calm this restless spirit.

My child, I asked for her, but they told me that I was not yet ready for her – although they let me see her through a veil. She was sitting in a garden; she appeared to be so much at peace with herself. I wept, for I wanted her forgiveness. I was told that she had forgiven me on the Earth plane, and that is why she was at peace, but yet, I forever tormented myself.

I was pleased with those Masters in the Spirit realms that they grant me a chance to return and to put the record straight, but I had to wait until the time was right. The time is now right for me to speak of the truth – My Truth.

My thoughts now have changed from those bitter words full of gall that I left behind all those centuries ago. So if they still exist, pray listen to what I have to say, for on reflection, they are now being addressed. Those papers are mine, and I do not wish them used for monetary or personal gain, and if they are, the reckoning will come to them, for they were not meant for prying eyes and should have been placed in my tomb when I was laid to rest.

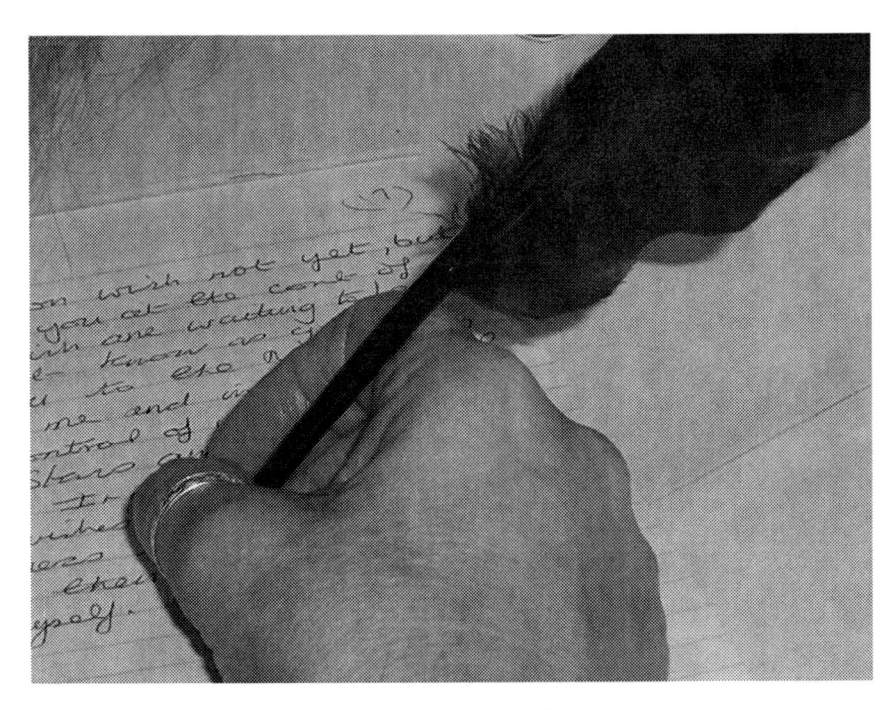

Brenda penning 'My Truth'
(Photograph by Neville Harwood)

Epilogue

This book is finished, but my story is not over, there is much I have to tell. My mind is in torment through the torture I endured while under arrest. I find it very painful to bring to mind all that happened to Thomas Kydd and myself.

The guilt I have carried all these years I will speak of in my next book. It will reveal my work in the continuous service of Robert Cecil and Her Majesty.

My esoteric knowledge shall I impart and tell of the only woman in my life whom I ever did love and trust and of the child she bore me. I was not able to be a true father, and this frustrated me at times. My frustrations of living in fear and not knowing if I will live tomorrow, but hoping that one day I would at least die in England, the land of my birth and the land which I loved so dearly. For I always felt that I was the supreme sacrifice on the altar of hypocrisy.

Kit Marlowe

Printed in the United States
210102BV00013B/37/A